Czesław: His Life Story

A Sad Story Told with a Smile

EDDIE SOTHEBY

About the Book

Czesław was born in 1926 to Helena and Piotr Sowinski, in Warsaw, Poland.

Helena had previously been married to one of Piotr's brothers and they had two children together, Władysław and Irena. Tragically Piotr's brother died.

Piotr had always been a close friend to Helena and his brother. His friendship with Helena turned to love and they married. He loved Helena's children as his own. Czesław was their child of the marriage . Czesław dearly loved his brother and sister.

Czesław was Czes to his friends and called Czesiek by his mother and father. In the Polish language, there are many affectionate ways of saying the same name, these are common diminutive names, for example, my name Edward, could be Edek, Edzio, Mundek, Munzio.

The family lived in a four-storey tenement block in Warsaw. Piotr worked as a Telegraphic engineer manager for Warsaw's Post and Telegraph office.

Czesław grew up surrounded by friends and had many of them. He loved to play out, much to Helena's despair.

Czesław had tragedies in his life prior to and during the life changing break-out of
World War II.

During the occupation of Poland, Czesław found an inner strength that he never realised he had. He lost school friends to a firing squad, he witnessed massacres in the streets of Warsaw and the cruelty in the Jewish Ghettos. He saw the Jews leaving Warsaw to be incarcerated in the concentration death camps.

Twelve months later, Czesław was taken away from his family to face life alone.

Piotr and another of his brothers with Czesław, age 2

Chapter 1

A young boy, 7 years old, big blue eyes, short light brown hair, combed to a fringe. Grey shorts, blue shirt, black scuffed shoes; typical school wear. Named Czesław, Czes to his friends, Czesiek to his mother and father.

Czesław, age 7

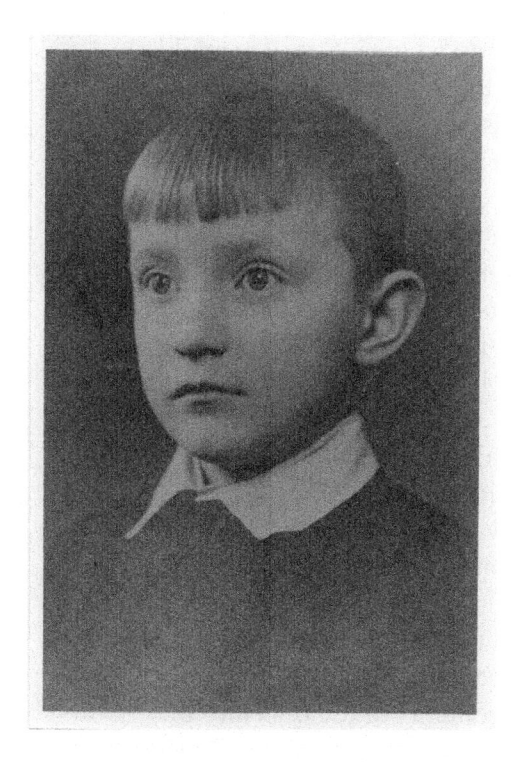

Czesław loved his family and friends, he liked the communal living in his block of tenement flats. They had open communal corridors that looked out onto the public space outside. The flats were situated in the city. Flat 19, Number 7, Przemysłowa. (Industry Street). This was a larger apartment than their previous one that they had lived in up until recently at number 30.

You could hear his shoes echo along the open balcony corridor, his footsteps resonated down the stairway as he descended to the ground floor, hands out in front of him to push the entrance door open. He burst through the doorway that led to the outside flagged and grassed area. Czesław could hear the bin wagon's loud engine as it laboured under the weight of its heavy load of waste collected from the Cities dwellings. The vehicle appeared through the gap between the flats leading from the main road, emitting black exhaust fumes at the rear. The wagon continued into the large cul-de-sac, carrying out its once weekly visit. There was a cluster of three identical brick block tenement flats served by the metalled tarmac turning area.

Czesław's happy high pitched young voice echoed off the surrounding blocks. He acknowledged the bin men clad in heavy wool jackets and blue overalls. They were busy running off in all directions and retrieving heavy dustbins full of domestic rubbish and the discarded ash from the open fires that warmed the apartments.

The men poured the contents of the bins into the rear of the Mercedes truck releasing large clouds of ash dust.

"Dzień dobry Pani" said Czesław.

One dust covered man acknowledged the young boy's greeting; he raised a hand in a friendly wave, a hand that was dark with soot and ash which had adhered to the sweat on his arms and face.

Czesław ran off leaving the noisy truck behind and ran through the narrow road exit between the large blocks of flats to the main road. These blocks had shops below them. He stood at the roadside looking at the stables and fields across the road. Czesław ran across the busy main road, remembering his mother's voice, "Look both ways before you cross Czesiek."

He had a red shiny apple in his left hand. He felt in his pocket with his free hand, searching for a small knife, which he had borrowed from the breakfast table. Czesław ran along the dirt track. The terrain fell gently into a dip with a raised mound to the right of the track. He ran up to the mound; the stable was just metres away. He stopped at the stable door with his prize in his left hand and small knife in his right hand. Czesław wiped his runny nose with the back of his hand. It was dripping with the exertion of running in the cold morning air. Steam vented from his mouth. A big brown horse heard him approach and clip-clopped towards the door; its hooves clattered as it turned and walked towards the split barn door where the doorways top half was already open.

"Morning Czes" said a cheery voice from deep inside the dark stable.

It was the stable boy, his face was always dirty; it

must have been dirt from his muddy hands. He was busy cleaning the stable, gathering up the steaming horse manure and straw with a long forked tool, lifting the heavy mass into a large barrow beside him.
"Morning Stefan" replied Czesław.
He held out his hand flat, fingers straight, just like his father had shown him, the fresh cut apple white side up on the palm of his hand. The horse sniffed at the offering, and gave a snort, then used its lips and tongue to take the cut piece of apple. Czesław wiped his now wet shiny palm on his grey school trousers and bit on the remaining half of the apple that he had kept for himself. Czesław stroked, then patted the large brown mane. It was time to go. Czesław shouted goodbye into the shadows where Stefan had been stood, no sign of him, Stefan must have been around the back of the stable emptying the contents of the barrow. Czesław turned and ran back down the track, startling the hens as he passed them on the way back to the main road. He turned left and headed for school. A horse drawn furniture wagon passed Czesław. He read the inscription out loud to himself. "Mindelshonn Warsaw Poland".

 The mist was clearing from the street opposite the school playground. People walked in and out of shops, doing what adults do. Wagons were being unloaded, deliveries of large boxes going in, customers buying and carrying large bags and boxes coming out of the shops.

Czesław felt a hand grab his ear, his attention returned to the classroom. He could feel the

cartilage of his tiny ear being crushed by Miss
Cichowska's large rough hand. She turned
Czesław's head towards the chalk board,
"I will write a note for you to take home to your
parents Czesław"
"Yes Miss Cichowska" chanted Czesław, as
children do in reply at school.
His friends Bernek, Janek, Waldek and Jurek
chatted excitedly around him on the way home.
Czesław was kicking a large piece of ice as if it
were a football.
"I want to be a footballer like my cousin Stanley"
said Czesław.
His friends did not hear him as they talked
excitedly about the skating they had all planned for
that evening. Czesław did not join in the
conversation, he was not looking forward to this
evening. He was going to be in trouble. Czesław
played with the note in his pocket, wondering if he
should just throw it away.
Czesław ran up the eight flights of communal
stairs at his tenement block, walking was boring.
He clattered through the apartment entrance door.
Helena was there cooking, preparing the evening
meal.
"Hi Mama" said Czesław .
Czesław kissed his mother and pushed the
envelope into her apron strings that were tied
around her waist with a tidy bow at the rear.
 "What's this Czesiek?" said Helena
She wiped her hands on the front of the apron,
before reaching behind her for the envelope that he
had tucked in to the strings near the bow. Czesław

ran out of the kitchen on a mission. He had seen his ice skates near the entrance door below the coat rack.

Helena shouted after him as he closed the apartment door quietly behind him, hoping not to be heard.

"Hurry back Czesiek your tea will be ready soon."

Czesław ran along the communal fourth floor corridor without a thought of what he may or may not have heard.

"Hi Jurek, I'm off skating, you coming too?"

"Yes coming, just let me get my skates. Czes, I thought you were staying in tonight?"

"Oh that, well, yes but, no but…."

"I'll be back for tea Mama," said Czesław half turning back in the direction of his mother's voice.

"Czesiek, kiss!" said Helena standing in the apartment doorway. She stood with the unread note in her right hand. Too late, he was already excitedly talking to his friend and running along the communal concrete balcony, shoes echoing on the concrete floor,

"Of course Mama" Czesław's voice echoed back as he headed for the stairs.

His mother called after him "Slow down Czesiek." Helena closed the door slowly, as mothers do, half regretting that he was growing up so quickly.

"Why can't time stand still?" she thought, as the door latch clicked securely into the catch in the doorframe.

Czesław acknowledged his wrinkly neighbour. How on earth she walked up the eight flights of steps of the tenement block was a mystery to

Czesław. She must have been fifty, but looked like a 100-year-old tortoise to young Czesław.
"I'm off skating Pani Kaminska."
"Slow down Czesiek." she said stopping to regain her breath "you will have an accident."
"Old people are so cautious" thought Czesław, as he held up his skates to show them off to her, then placed them back over his right shoulder, like he imagined professional skaters would do.
"Not so fast Czesiek" said a deeper voice.
A wall of black appeared blocking the stairway.
A smart looking young man appeared on the stairway, dressed in a black suit with a warm woollen black long coat, unbuttoned and open at the front. It was Czesław's father. Piotr worked as a Telegraphic engineer manager at Warsaw's Post and Telegraph office. He had walked up the stairway, no panting, hardly any effort; he was a fit young man. He rubbed his thin moustache with his index finger as he looked down at his young son.
"Hi Tata I'm off skating to the park."
"Have fun, be careful little man."
"Will do Tata."
"No kiss for your father?" said Piotr in mock disbelief.
Czesław was in a rush. No time to reply to his father.
"Wait!" Piotr shouted. Piotr held out his closed hand, "Buy something while you're out."
"Okay Dzięki Tata," Czesław's voice echoed and sounded from the stairwell as he continued his run, footsteps clattering down the stairway.
Czesław was jumping down the last four steps on

each flight of stairs, bending his knees on impact as he landed with a thud. Hands out in front as he burst out through the glass paned door out into the cold air, followed closely by Jurek.
Their breath hung in a cloud. Czesław's eyes searched for their friends that they were meeting for this evening's skate.
"Waldek!" Czesław shouted. He had seen one of his best friends amongst a group of boys in the communal circle area. "Let's go. I'm going to skate until I can skate no more tonight" said Czesław.
"You and me both Czes" said Waldek.

The excited group of youngsters were now five in number. Excited 10-year-old boys running down the icy path like only children can do without breaking a limb.
The street lights glowed on the soft laying snow beneath them, the surface of the snow glistening. Diamond like sparkles from the frost forming on the snow covered ground. A magical scene that you would only notice with older, mature eyes; this show of brilliance was wasted on the boys. Running down the street was effortless, legs carried along with happy laughter and jokes that made little sense, but were hilarious to the happy group of young boys. Life was good, exciting, the boys had the rest of their lives ahead of them. They were emerging from behind the apron strings of their proud adoring mothers, growing up to be little individuals; the young men of Warsaw.
As they entered the park through the Municipal gates, the park manager shouted after them,

"Stay off the grass and everyone out of the park on time this evening!"

The park manager's face creased with a frown. The sight of the happy group reminded him of himself as a child visiting the park with his friends, "Young kids, what do they know?" A tear glistened in his eye, hardly perceivable in the dim street lighting. He had lost many of his good friends in the war; it was known as The War to him. Little did he know that his war was going to be the first of two world wars.

Music could be heard in waves, little bursts of sound carried on the cold night air from piano accordions. The instrument had a French connection dating back to Napoleon's rule of Poland. Poland is the only country in the world to invoke Napoleon in its national anthem. The Polish people welcomed the Napoleonic forces as liberators. This was before the partitioners, Russia, Austria and Germany's occupation of Poland. Polish independence was not gained until the end of the First World War. Poland has a rich history of occupation. The melodies could be heard more clearly as the group approached the fields where the crowds had gathered.

The park manager had poured gallon upon gallon of water onto the playing fields in the weeks leading up to the first frosts. This created a natural ice rink in the municipal park. Lights were festooned on the trees that surrounded the skating area. The lights lit the ice, making a magical winter scene. A group of young girls from Czesław's school giggled when they saw the panting sweating bright red faced group of boys running towards them.

One girl from the group shouted "Czes, see if you and your boys can catch us."

"Wait, I need to put my skates on first" Czesław chuckled.

Winter evenings were so much fun. Czesław remembered his mother and father teaching him to skate at the park when he was a young child. His parents used to hold a hand each as Czesław skated between them. They went so fast together that his eyes would fill up and water in the cold crisp air. He remembered giggling until his sides hurt.

Czesław's cold fingers could not work fast enough tonight on the ice skate laces, they were chilled by the crisp icy cold odourless air.

Czesław was so excited; it was the first outing for his shiny new skates.

"I'll be the fastest tonight, you'll see! With my new skates on, I will fly" said Czesław.

Piotr had saved up over the months to buy Czesław his new skates as a Christmas present. Czesław had admired the shiny pair of skates through a glass pane. The pane of glass used to steam up under his warm breath. Nose pushed up against the glass of the shop window, leaving a smudge print from his button nose. The polished black boots with shiny silver blades stood proud, enticing Czesław to look in the window every time he passed with his father.

"You would have to be very well behaved and do well at school to receive such beautiful skates for Christmas" said Piotr.

"Could I Tata? I will be so good this year, on my best behaviour ever!"

Piotr looked down at his excited little boy as they stood in the Stare Miasto square, in Warsaw's beautiful Old Town.

Piotr had a good salary working for the Warsaw Post Office communications. Morse code and telegrams were the fast messaging service of the time. Cables below the sea were not a success at this stage and instead wireless communication transmitted by radio waves was used for transatlantic calls using Morse code. The messages were received at the telegraphic offices, where the young apprentice telecommunication boys called telegram delivery boys would collect the decoded messages and deliver them to the public using bicycles and later small motor bikes.

Helena had said the skates were a bit more than they could afford. "Czesiek should use his old skates until his feet stop growing" said Helena. Piotr carefully and diplomatically put his case forward to Helena,

"Helena, Czesiek is young. Who knows what the future holds for the young ones these days? I've been through the Great War and learnt that we should all live for the day, not the future."

Her expression softened, as Piotr brushed her cheek with his hand. Helena could see the severed stump of his little finger on his right hand that had been destroyed by shrapnel from an exploding hand grenade in the War. Helena reached out and held his hand tightly against her cheek. Helena was not afraid of this war scar, she instead saw it as the

mark of his heroism and a recognition of the pain and suffering their country's people had been through in their fight for freedom in recent times.
"You're right Piotr, now is what is important." conceded Helena.
They embraced in a way that couples do that are comfortable in each other's arms, a brief moment that says I'm here for you. Piotr broke away first, walking over to the fireplace.
"I'll place some more coal on the fire, it is going to be cold tonight."
Czesław was ready to go, skates on, wearing a cheeky grin as he saw the young girls speed past him again, waving and giggling. There must have been his entire school class out at the park tonight.
"Come on Bernek, let's race!" said Czesław.
The boys joined the existing group of disciplined skaters, who were following a regular anti-clockwise circuit around the ice. Czesław and the boys weaved between the skaters like a group of dolphins invading a shoal of mackerel. Tuts and raised eyebrows were left in the wake of the speedy group of young boys.
 When the boys caught up with the girls there were jokes and a couple of gentle tugs on the long tied-back hair of the girls in front of them. Playful pushes and side-steps, all the way around the ice between the group of friends.
"Let's get a drink" said Czesław.
"I've no money" said Waldek.
"Well I have some" said Czesław patting his pocket with his gloved hand.
"My tata said we should get something while we

are out in the park."
He felt in his coat pocket for the coins his father had handed him on the stairway at home.
Inside the tearoom it felt so hot after the minus figures out on the rink. The wooden building echoed with excited voices of children and adults sat eating treats and drinking hot drinks.
Hot chocolate was the order of the day. Czesław and his friends joined the queue, their red cheeks glowed like the red apple that Czesław had fed the large brown horse that morning. His skin prickled as sweat broke through the pores on the surface of his hot skin. The group of friends looked up in anticipation at the counter where a lady took their order, she then turned to a rear worktop to prepare their hot drinks. Hot chocolate had never smelt or tasted so good. It tasted like the hot chocolate, gorąca czekoladay, at the Wedel café, on Szpitalna Street in Warsaw. Helena and Piotr took Czesław to Wedel's cafe every birthday. He would be going there again soon, his birthday was next month, the 27th of February. His 11th Birtday.
The staff at Wedel's always fussed over Czesław. Wedel's was really well decorated inside; polished wooden floors and pinky red walls which matched the folding sun canopies that were above every window on the outside of the ground floor tenement block. Wedel's had been there since Czesław's father Piotr was a boy. Piotr used to go there with his father, Jan for birthday treats.
Like all good things do, the evening's skating was all too quickly coming to an end. The park keeper and café staff would be ready to go home.

Farewells were said at the end of the evening. Czesław gave a friendly final tug to the pony tail of the girl that had teased him on the ice. Kristina got her revenge by tripping Czesław up with a well-placed boot around his ankle, Czesław rolled on the ground and jumped to his feet quickly with an exaggerated *Ta Da* pose with his arms widely spread like a gymnast completing a routine. This performance was greeted with hysterical giggles from the group of friends around him. Czesław dusted off the dry crisp snow from his trousers and coat.
"Yes I'll take that one Kristina" laughed Czesław.
"See you at school tomorrow"
"No you won't, it's Saturday" said Kristina.
"Lucky me" said Czesław, "I won't have to see your face tomorrow after all Kristina."
More giggles as they parted. The group set off, running towards the park gates where the friendly park keeper stood.
"Kids!" said the park keeper with a smile.

Chapter 2

Czesław was excited he was going to watch Stanley Yablonski, his Mother's nephew, play football at the Warsaw stadium. Stanley was so good that he was being paid to play football now. Czesław loved Stanley like an uncle. Stanley was about 10 years older than Czesław, his blond hair combed in a natural wave across his head. He was broad, tall and strong. Stanley had given three free entry tickets to Czesław, Piotr and Władysław. Władysław was Czesław's maternal half-brother, Helena's son. Free tickets to the Skra Stadium in Warsaw was a dream come true for Czesław. This was Czesław's first visit to a proper football match in a stadium. Czesław felt special going through the turnstiles into the stadium to watch Stanley and his team. They made their way along with the crowd. They stood momentarily together in the entrance to the Western stand, Czesław stood rooted to the spot in stunned silence, in awe of the incredibly vast area in front of him. Czesław had never seen an area with so many people in the same place. Czesław, Piotr and Władysław all cheered and shouted together when Stanley's team ran onto the pitch. Strong athletic young men. Stanley was at the front. Stanley knew that Czesław was in the West Stand, so he skipped and turned towards the stand and waved to where he thought Czesław and his family would be stood. Stanley could not see Czesław, but he knew Czesław would see him waving to him. Czesław

was beside himself when he saw Stanley.
"Look Tata, Stanley is waving at us."
All three of them cheered together and shouted back to Stanley.

The game was full of excitement; Stanley scored a goal in the first ten minutes of the game. Czesław cheered and jumped with joy.
"We are going to win Władysław" said Czesław, his face beaming with delight.
The team ran off the pitch at half time, 1-0 in front. Stanley waved again to the West stand, Czesław was jumping for joy again in response to Stanley.
"When they come back on, they have to win, I can't bear the tension" said Czesław.
The opposing team had heeded a half-time pep talk. They were off at the whistle with possession of the ball deep into the opposition's territory. The young attacking striker ran down towards the penalty box and jumped over Stanley's leg, as Stanley had committed himself to a sliding tackle, in a brave attempt to get the ball away from the determined forward. Still the player was not stopped and he continued his run, outpacing two other defenders. He stopped, looked up and found his team mate at the far side of the goal mouth. A chip across and a well-placed boot brought the score to one-all.
"Oh no!" said Czesław looking through his fingers that he had hidden his face with. The opposing team supporters were going wild with joy. Piotr and Władysław looked at poor Czesław.
Disappointment is even harder to handle when you are young. Age helps you to understand that not

everything goes the way you want it to.
"Chin up Czesiek, there is lots of time left" said Władysław, as he placed his strong hand on Czesław's hair and ruffled it up.
"Maybe we will be okay," said Czesław.
Only three minutes of the game remained. Czesław's voice was breaking up, he had never shouted so loud and for so long without his father correcting him. Stanley ran forward collecting the ball from a well-placed throw in from the side line.
"Go Stanley!" shouted all three men in unison. Stanley looked forward and saw an unmarked team player on the far left of the pitch. He stopped, looked forward again and without once looking at the ball, kicked the heavy leather bound ball to his team mate, striking it high. Stanley then immediately ran to the right side of the pitch making a heroic sprint. "He is creating space" said Władysław.
"What's that?" said Czesław
"Watch closely" said Władysław.
Stanley saw his team mate controlling the ball. He was moving forward, then feigned to the side on his left leg, only to reverse which produced its desired effect by pulling in two, then three defenders, he was drawing the defenders towards himself, he knew exactly where Stanley would be, they had both practiced this set piece all week. At the last second Stanley ran forward into the penalty box, taking the distracted defenders by surprise. The team mate with the ball, who was surrounded by defenders, looked up and kicked the ball over to the right side of the penalty box where Stanley was

racing to.

"Now watch Czesiek, the final part of the jigsaw" said Władysław.

 Stanley was running as fast as he could to beat the distracted defenders. They did not see the attack coming from the opposite side of the goal mouth. It all went into slow motion at this point. Stanley leapt into the air to intercept the heavy leather clad bladder moving fast through the air. His head came into contact with the ball in midair, the laces on the ball that held the ball's internal bladder in place struck Stanley's forehead hard. He turned the direction of the ball towards the top right corner of the goal. The referee didn't know if he should look at his watch or the game; they were within the last minute of play. The ball was on target, Stanley was still in midair together with the goal keeper, whose arms were outstretched, all eyes fixed on the leather bound sphere. Czesław arms were rising involuntarily up into the air, Władysław and Piotr were mirroring Czesław's movement in unison. The goal keeper's fingers strained, outstretched, his eyes focussed on the projectile, like a hunting eagle trying to catch its prey. The goal keeper's finger tips came briefly into contact with the ball, his fingers started to bend back with the force of the well placed header. The ball glanced slightly with the contact from the goal keeper's fingers, its trajectory became erratic and wobbled, continuing its way to the top right corner of the goal. The keeper began to succumb to the earth's pull of gravity, as he began his descent towards the hard ground. Stanley was also returning to terra firma, both had their eyes fixed in the direction of the spinning ball as they fell.

"Gooooaaal!" shouted Czesław jumping up and down.

The three of them were all stood with heads high and arms aloft. The shrill *peep* of the referee's whistle sounded for the end of the game; its sound was almost drowned out by the crowd's cheers.

"We did it!" exclaimed Czesław "We won. Stanley is a hero!"

The crowd around them were all jumping up and down enjoying the moment shouting until their voices gave out.

"This is one of the best days of my life" said Czesław.

It was one of those occasions that they would all remember forever.

Monday came all too quickly. Czesław was looking out of the window daydreaming, replaying the exciting moments of the football match in his head, the noise of the cheering was all so real, as if he was still at the Skra stadium. Czesław heard a shout from someone stood next to his chair. Before he could turn his head away from the window, he felt a familiar hand wrap around his ear lobe, the coarse skin, not gentle and soft like the touch from his mother's hand. He felt burning as the intimidating Miss Cichowska again had the cartilage of his ear in her tight grip. The other hand was placed in front of him on the desk, Czesław looked down and noticed the dark blue veins of her hand standing up to attention. His eyes slowly adjusted from the bright light of outside the

window, to the image of his teacher in the classroom. Her face came in to view as she lowered her head, looking into Czesław's big blue startled eyes.
"Caught you daydreaming, again!" shouted Miss Cichowska.
As she shouted at Czesław, spittle projected from her flapping lips, rather like a fish out of water and splashed Czesław on the cheek. Punctuating every word with a splash of Miss Cichowska's spit. Czesław did not dare brush the wet spittle away until Miss Cichowska released his ear, he did not want the pain to be prolonged a second longer by upsetting his teacher by any further actions on his part.
 At the end of the class Miss Cichowska made Czesław stay behind and stand at her desk while she scratched yet another hand written letter addressed to his parents. She slowly and precisely folded the letter, pressing down on each crease with exaggerated force. Czesław looked at Miss Cichowska as she performed her task. The effort of pressing down on the paper made her grunt with the exertion. The teacher handed over the letter, arm outstretched to where Czesław stood at the side of the long desk.
"Take!"
"Thank you Miss Cichowska" said Czesław in the chanting voice.
Miss Cichowska shooed him away with her hand, as if he was a pungent smell.
Czesław walked out of school slowly almost dragging his heels, he was not looking forward to

arriving home tonight, yet another letter; this would upset his parents.
Waldek turned to Czesław.
"Come on slow coach! You are walking so slowly tonight."
"You go on ahead" said Czesław.
Waldek acknowledged him with a wave of his hand and left Czesław in his world of pain.
"See you later slow coach" he said.
Waldek quickened his pace to a trot. He turned around to face Czesław and continued a fast trot backwards with exaggerated knees up. This made Czesław laugh.
"At last!" said Waldek laughing with Czesław.
"I'm playing out after I've finished my homework" said Waldek, "I hope you are allowed out too."
"We'll see" replied Czesław, not holding out any hope of that happening tonight.
Czesław clutched the school letter even tighter in his hand. It reminded Czesław of the trauma to his right ear. He rubbed the throbbing ear involuntarily with his free hand.
Czesław reached the tenement block entrance. His home was not as inviting as usual. This was his second letter in as many weeks. Czesław knew he would be punished. Helena and Piotr took education very seriously. Czesław knew that even though his father loved him dearly, there would be a beating tonight. Czesław walked slowly up the four storey block of steps, two flights per floor, as he counted the steps in his head. He felt like a condemned man, just like in the stories he had read. He imagined what it would be like walking

to the gallows. Czesław tried to imagine what it must feel like knowing that you only had moments to live.

Czesław slowly pushed open the apartment door. He could hear movement in the kitchen, his mother was busy making the evening meal for them.

"You're late home today Czesiek" said Helena in a concerned tone.

"Yes Mama."

"What's wrong Czesiek?"

"Are you in a good mood Mama?" asked Czesław hesitantly.

"Why, what have you done now Czesiek?"

Czesław handed over the letter, stepped back and held his breath, eyes tightly closed, all in anticipation of the reaction to come.

The touch paper was lit..."Stand well back" thought Czesław. Helena read the letter, her face changed from her usual smile..."and there she blows!"

Helena, in a flash of rage turned and grabbed the tea towel that hung on the handle of the oven range. Czesław stepped backwards and turned. Helena chased a fleeing Czesław around and around the kitchen table. Czesław half turned midflight and tried to kiss his mother's hands as she chased him hitting him with the tea towel. The tea towel did not hurt, but the shouting hurt Czesław a lot more. Czesław was sad that he had upset and disappointed his mother.

"Go to your room Czesiek and wait until your father comes home."

"Yes Mama" said Czesław.

He grabbed and kissed his mother's hands again, while saying "sorry Mama" over and over before he left to go to his room.
Czesław opened his satchel and pulled out his school books; they were all very tidy and clean. Czesław took great pride in keeping his things nice and tidy. With a heavy sigh he laid on the bed on his tummy, knees bent, feet up in the air behind him. For the first time in ages, he was concentrating hard on his school books, even if it was just to pass the time.
After what seemed a lifetime of waiting, Czesław heard the apartment door open,
"Hello Helena" said a happy to be home voice. It was Piotr.
"I've bought a record that I know you'll like Helena."
Piotr and Helena loved their music collection. Czesław cracked open his bedroom door ever so quietly, so that he could hear the exchange of greetings between his mother and father. Then the conversation became quieter so he could not easily hear what they were saying. Czesław stepped out of his room and strained to hear, mouth open. That always helped him hear better, something to do with not hearing the blood circulation in your head when your mouth is open. Then came a rapid outburst by his mother, to which Piotr replied
"This is the third letter this month from school."
"Third?" said Czesław out loud. "I thought it was the second. Now I'm really for it," he thought.
Before Czesław had time to retreat to his room, he heard his father's voice, "Czesław!" shouted Piotr.

His Sunday name was being used. That was not a good sign thought Czesław.
 "Czesław I have the letter from your teacher. You have not been paying attention at school…again!"
Czesław closed his bedroom door and dived under his blankets. He rubbed his eyes and threw some water from the glass on his bedside cabinet into his eyes. He needed to look repentant. Czesław heard footsteps approaching. The steps stopped outside of his room. Piotr politely and gently knocked on Czesław's bedroom door. To Czesław at this moment in time, the knock sounded like thunder.
"Come in Papa" said a muffled voice from under the bed sheets.
Piotr opened the door and saw the mound which was Czesław under the blankets. Piotr quietly said "Come down to the kitchen Czesław."
Czesław hesitantly entered the kitchen, where both his parents stood. They were silent and both looking directly at him. There was no usual friendly greeting, no usual smiles. Piotr stood near the white pot sink, next to his shaving strop which he used to polish and straighten the blade of his straight blade shaving razor. Helena was stood further to the left near the cooker, she turned away pretending to busy herself stirring the lovely creamy soup that Czesław loved to eat on a cold winter's evening. The lovely homely smell of celery and potato filled the room.
Czesław's father walked to where Czesław stood.
"Go and touch the strop Czesław" said Piotr, pointing to the leather strop hung on a nail adjacent to the sink.

"This letter informs me that you are not behaving well at school."
"I'm so sorry Father, I will behave better." said a repentant Czesław.
"This is the third time this month" said Piotr.
Piotr's tone was measured and deeper than usual.
"Smell the strop...smell it!" said Piotr.
"I will punish you this evening before bedtime. You will now gather your school books from your room and you will do your school work supervised by your mother in this kitchen."
Piotr left them both in the kitchen. Czesław looked up again at the strop hung on the wall. It was really scary.
Czesław was working through his school books. Helena left the pans simmering and sat down next to Czesław at the kitchen table. Helena could not keep the anger thing going as she saw his eyes closing, his head nodding, in the warm cozy humidity of the kitchen.
"Close your eyes Czesiek take a 10 minute nap. Then you can start your school work again later." Helena stood up and walked over to the kitchen door and pushed it closed, she did not want Piotr to see Czesław asleep. The door opened again almost immediately, quietly, Piotr's head appeared, he gave a warm smile and winked his eye at Helena. Helena felt burning behind her eye lids and then the cooling tears bathed her eyes. She smiled back at Piotr blinking away the tears. The tears were not out of sadness, they were from an inexplicable feeling of intense love for her family. Czesław soon awoke, unaware and continued his homework

refreshed after his cat nap. His mother often told Czesław to take short naps. He always felt so much better after them.
After a lot of head scratching and writing, he had completed his school work. "Finished Mama."
"Lovely, now clear away your books and your Father and I will prepare the table.
They all sat down together to enjoy their evening meal, no further references were made to the strop. After the meal Piotr and Helena washed, dried and tidied away the crockery. Czesław went into the sitting room and placed a record onto the record deck.He could hear his mother and father singing to the music of the record playing. Czesław smiled and felt happy inside again.
Piotr and Helena came into the room together.
"I'll put the new record on Czesiek that I brought home this evening for your mother."
Piotr gently lowered the record deck arm down to the record. There was a crackle as the needle touched the record, there was a slight delay as the needle followed the groove and moved on to where the music started.
"That is beautiful" said Helena. "It really is."
Piotr walked over to Helena and they danced a dance called the Tango. The Tango was introduced to Poland in 1913, with the performance of Victor Jacobi's opera Targ na Dziewczęta (Girls Market) at the New Theatre in Warsaw. The music was very popular and often heard on the radio and played on gramophone records. The record playing was by Arthur Gold and his cousin Jerzy Petersburski, one of the most renowned dance

orchestras in Warsaw.

Czesław watched his parents dance. They were good. Czesław applauded when they finally stopped. As it got later Czesław got ready for bed and was kissed on the head by Helena.

"I will come to see you when you are in bed Czesław" said Helena.

Czesław got himself ready, washed his face and teeth, then called from his bedroom to say he was ready.

"Mama and Tata."

Czesław got into bed and turned out the light. There was a gentle knock at his bedroom door.

"Proszę" said Czesław.

"Proszę" said Piotr.

Piotr cracked the door open. Czesław lay quietly, apprehensive. Piotr walked in quietly and gently lowered himself and sat on the bed.

"We want you to do well at school Czesiek. It is very important to get a good education." Piotr turned and looked in to Czesław's wet and runny eyes.

"You will be able to apply for a job at the Post Office, at the offices where I work when you complete all your levels at school. Is that still what you want to do Czesiek?"

"More than anything Tata, I want a good job like you so that I can look after my family one day like you do."

Piotr leant forward and kissed him on the head.

"Sleep well Czesiek"

"Night night Tata, kocham cię. "

"Kocham cię Czesiek."

The next morning everything was as normal.
"Morning Czesiek" said Piotr. "Do well at school. I will see you both this evening."
Piotr kissed Helena on the cheek and then kissed Czesław on the crown of his head. Piotr turned and left for work
"Love you both" said Piotr as he left the apartment.
"Love you too Tata" shouted Czesław.

Front row, left to right: Piotr and Helena (Czesław's parents) and Vanda (Piotr's sister)

Back row, left to right: Alodia, Anna (Stanley's mother) and Barbara (Stanley's sister)

Chapter 3

"Piotr, may I speak to you."
"Yes, come on into the office Edziu."
Edziu was a plump man, not very tall, about 1.5 metres in height and almost as wide, he sported a comb over and looked older than his 40 years. They had both worked together since they joined the Post Office of Warsaw as young messenger boys on bicycles back in the day. Piotr was Edziu's manager now. They had a friendship going back to before they started work together. School friends and play pals.
 "We have some puppy dogs. One would be ideal for your młody syn, Czesiek."
 "Thank you Edziu , I'll call over this evening to look at them if I may?" said Piotr
 "My young son would love a puppy. Dziękuję Ci Edziu."
Piotr returned home that evening with a small white bundle of fur. The puppy was hidden, tucked inside his coat.
He made sure the puppy could not be seen as he opened the apartment door.
"I have a surprise for you both" said Piotr as he removed his wide brimmed hat with his free hand, the other kept tight hold of his coat lapels, so as to keep the little bundle covered up, he hung the hat on a hat hook.
Helena appeared in the hallway drying her hands on her apron. "What have you got for us Piotr?"

said Helena leaning forward for a kiss on the cheek.

"Is Czesiek in?" asked Piotr. He found it hard to keep the surprise a secret any longer.

"Czesiek is out as usual, you will have to show me" said Helena, intrigued by Piotr's secrecy.

The apartment door burst open behind them.

"Mama ,Tata I'm back, in a big rush tonight, football at the back of the tenements, big game, there are boys from across the street coming to play tonight..."

Piotr stopped Czesław mid-sentence with his surprise. Piotr reached in to the open V of his big black coat and pulled out a wriggling excited ball of white fur. A high pitched bark sounded from the fluffy white fur ball. A tiny puppy bark.

"Aww it is piękny" said Czesław."

" Yes Czesiek it is truly beautiful" agreed Helena.

"Oh, how, where, what's the puppy doing here?" asked Czesław in a state of shock.

"It's yours Czesiek. Well, if your mother approves of course" said Piotr looking across at Helena for her approval.

"I only found out about the puppy today Helena, honestly, otherwise I would have asked you first"

Helena looked at the little ball of fur and then at her two men, "I can hardly say no now."

"May I hold him?" asked a very excited Czesław

"Of course, he is for you Czesiek"

The little furry white face looked up and focused on Czesław's smiling face. Their eyes met and there were hugs and puppy kisses. It was delightful being licked, this was nowhere near as bad as being licked by the rough rasping tongue of the big brown horse at the stables.

"Who will look after the little Rascal?" questioned Helena.

Helena knew she would end up looking after the puppy.

"Czesiek will look after him. Look at them both, they are made for each other" said Piotr

"Where is it from?" asked Helena pretending not to be interested in the little bundle.

"A colleague, Edziu, you know, with the comb over, at work. He and his wife were going to drown it in the Vistula tonight, it's the last of the litter." explained Piotr

Czesław stood gazing in horror, the thought of Edziu drowning the poor little ball of fluff in the river made him feel sad.

Piotr winked at Czesław as if to be forgiven for his little white lie to Helena. Czesław laughed when he caught the joke.

Helena was horrified, "Oh no, we can't let them do that to the poor little Skrawek"

"Skrawek it is. Yes, let's call him Scrap, that's a great name Mama. Oh little Skrawek you are godny podziwu" said Czesław

"Yes he is adorable Czesiek." Piotr agreed

Helena watched the puppy and boy together.

"It is true unconditional love." said Piotr.

"It really is Piotr, and I know how they feel" said Helena looking into the eyes of her kind, loving husband.

"So you are not cross with me Helena that I did not consult with you on the matter of the puppy?"

"No, it's fine. It's more than fine, it's lovely." said Helena.

"Oh and Czesiek another good thing. You can show Skrawek to Irena. She is coming to see us tonight and I know how much you love to see your sister. Now off to your football, we will look after the little Skrawek for you" said Helena.

Irena was Czesław's half-sister, Helena's daughter from her previous marriage to Piotr's brother. Piotr's brother had tragically died, leaving behind Irena and son Władysław. Czesław was Piotr's and Helena's son together since their marriage.

Czesław burst out of the apartment onto the communal landing, he ran along the corridor and greeted 'Mrs. Tortoise face' with a happy smile.

"We have a new puppy" said Czesław.

"Well don't let it wee in my doorway" was the rebuke to Czesław, as she smiled to herself.

Czesław did not even hear the reply, his excited feet felt like they were flying, "I'm skipping for joy" thought Czesław.

Later that evening, after the football game, Czesław headed for home, football under his arm, his knees covered in mud, his head glistening with sweat.

Czesław burst in through the apartment door calling for little Skrawek.

Irena was already there.

Irena (Czesław's sister)

"How's my little brother?" asked Irena.
"Great, but a bit sweaty."
"I'm not worried about a bit of sweat Czesiek."
They both hugged. Czesław loved Irena dearly, she was 15 years older than Czesław, and he loved her like a second mother. Irena always made a big fuss of him.
"Kocham Cię" said Irena to Czesław,
"I love you too Irena." said Czesław.
"Have you seen Skrawek Irena?"
"Yes he is lovely, he's in the kitchen with Mother" said Irena. "I think Mother is giving him some treats."
The little scrap barked and entered the lounge followed by Helena. Skrawek slipped on the tiled floor as he ran, then tumbled over as he gained traction on the rug.
"Ha…he's just like you Czesiek" laughed his adoring sister.
"Why's that?" asked Czesław
"You both run around everywhere in a rush and fall over. You are both little puppies in my eyes" Irena laughed.
Her laughter was like music to Czesław's ears. Irena was always happy, full of life. Helena placed her hand gently on Irena's dark brown hair. Her hair turned under at the nape of her neck. Irena smiled, her big brown eyes smiled as much as her mouth did.
 Czesław smiled back. Czesław always noticed that Irena had a natural pout to her lips, just like the ladies in the movies he thought.
 Irena took a deep breath and then looked at her

mother and step-father. She had something to tell them.

Piotr was standing next to Helena, his arm around her they were both watching the chaotic scene of puppy and young son playing together with their gentle and kind daughter laughing at the chaotic scene before her. They were enjoying watching the fun. Piotr loved Irena as if she was his own daughter.

"I have good news, I'm expecting a baby!" said Irena excitedly.

"Congratulations Irena. We must celebrate. A toast for the new baby!" said Piotr

"I'm so happy for you my dear" said Helena walking over to where Irena was sat. She gave Irena a tight squeeze then held her daughter close. Czesław helped his father with the glasses, they were kept with the best plates in a glass display cabinet in the sitting room. Piotr poured a red liquid into the tiny glasses. The bottle made a glug, glug, glug sound as it filled the glasses. Cherry and vodka, it smelt divine. Czesław was allowed a small drop.

"Tastes like spicy cherry." said Czesław.

They all laughed. The future seemed so certain, it seemed so good.

The months passed and Irena's bump got noticeably larger every time they saw her. Her face became rounder and her dark brown hair got even thicker.

Chapter 4

Czesław, Piotr and Helena were all together in the kitchen working with Czesław on his homework. They were startled by a loud, urgent knock at the door. Piotr stood up from the table and walked to the door. Czesław and Helena could hear low voices talking. Helena could not wait any longer, her curiosity made her join Piotr at the door. Piotr turned to Helena.
"Irena is ready to give birth."
 Everything suddenly became a rush,
"Czesiek, I'm going to Irena's" said Helena
"Can I come too?"
"No, stay here with your father. I will go alone."
 Helena looked for her handbag, grabbed it and swung it over her shoulder. She unhooked her coat from the rack and placed it over her arm, then stepped through the doorway and left with Irena's next door neighbour.
They both walked along the walkway chatting excitedly. Czesław thought they looked like two giggling school girls. Helena remembered to turn and wave before she disappeared down the stairway. She blew a kiss, first to Czesław then to Piotr. Then she was gone.
 "We will go over to Irena's later on this evening Czesiek." said Piotr, as the two women disappeared out of view down the stairwell.

Helena arrived at Irena's, quite out of breath. They had both walked quickly and had not stopped chatting all the way. It was not the exercise that was affecting Helena, it was the excitement and worry of the fast approaching birth.

Helena thanked the neighbour, who left her at Irena's door. Helena knocked on the door.
A flustered, panicking husband answered the door to her. His cheeks were bright red and he was hyperventilating too.
 "Fear not, I'm here. Is the midwife here yet?" said Helena with her calming voice. She needed to take charge of the situation immediately.
"Not yet, she…she's on her way" stuttered Irena's terrified husband.

Helena busied herself to prepare the bedroom, towels in place, boiling sterile water in a bowl, clean towels. Husband banned from the bedroom, he had to go sit in the lounge well out of the way. This was women's business, no men required here. The nurse arrived and clip clopped in her court shoes across the linoleum, bag in hand and an already stained white apron; stained with blood from a previous baby delivery.

Piotr eventually put down his newspaper and called to Czesław.
"Come along, let's go across to Irena's and see how the baby situation is progressing."
The men all sat together in the lounge. They could hear moans and some stifled screams from the bedroom. There were voices of encouragement too.

Several hours passed before a baby's cry was heard from the bedroom. A baby girl was born into the world. Irena cradled her new baby, she had tears of joy in her eyes; her love for her daughter was overwhelming and she was sure her heart would burst. Helena popped her head around the sitting room door and called Irena's husband to join the group in the bedroom.
"Not long now Czesiek. Let's give them a bit of time to be together." said Piotr to Czesław.
Soon after, Helena appeared at the sitting room door again, her face was radiant, she looked so happy. Czesław thought his mother looked even younger than usual, no frown lines on her face at all, she looked truly happy.

Piotr and Helena congratulated the young couple on the new arrival. Czesław noticed that Irena's face was very red and hot. The nurse was trying to cool her forehead with a damp flannel. Irena smiled at Czesław.
"You are an uncle Czesiek."
Czesław was so excited, he wanted this moment to last forever, for time to stand still, they were all so happy together.

The day was very still, not a breath of a breeze. A bird sang a couple of beautiful tuneful notes high above in the tree that gently shaded the large group of people gathered together. They all looked very sad, they all focused on one place, on one thing. The tree was showing its first signs of light green leaves and buds. The sombre group below its

leaves were all smartly dressed in black, shaded by the trees branches. The sun tried to reach them through the branches and the new early spring leaves. The sun helped to warm the solemn group, who were stood close together. A baby was heard to chuckle as her father held her close, he squeezed her tightly into his long black coat. Tears rolled down his cheeks and some fell onto her tiny cheek.
"Let me help you" said Helena.
 Helena held out her visibly shaking hands to hold her granddaughter.
This was the saddest day of Czesław's life, so far. He thought it would never be possible to be happy again.
The wooden casket made of polished oak with large shiny brass handles was lowered into a black, deep hole. "If you were to topple over you would not be able to climb out of the hole" thought Czesław.

Ropes were held by four strong men; the men performing the task showed no emotion, they did not feel the pain of the surrounding onlookers, this was their job.
The coffin appeared to float as it was gently, slowly, lowered into the dark cold grave. The brass name plate reflected in the sunlight.
"Goodbye my lovely sister." said Czesław quietly.
Czesław was passed soil on a platter and he watched as others dropped the lumps of soil onto the polished wood casket. Czesław tried to aim away from the shiny wood, he did not want to scratch the polished wood lid of the coffin with his

lump of earth.

Irena had sadly not recovered from an infection that she had contracted at the birth of her little girl; her red hot cheeks had never cooled down.

Chapter 5

Summer was approaching. The heat from the sun was getting stronger day by day. The trees' leaves changed from the light green of spring to the full lush dark green of the new season. The daylight lasted late on into the evening. Czesław gazed out of the apartment windows at the trees, summer camp would soon be upon him. He hated going away from home, having to leave Skrawek, his friends and mother and father. Czesław went to summer camp in Szczyrk. A town in the Beskid Śląski Mountains of southern Poland in the valley of the Żylica River, a place of great beauty. Piotr organised it through the Post Office of Warsaw where he worked. The government used to provide recreation and leisure for their employees for just a small contribution; summer camps for children, sanatoriums for adults. The sanatoriums were a place to go and relax and improve your health away from the city. Piotr used to book a week away for himself at the sanatoriums every year. Helena was not interested, she was more like Czesław and she liked to be at home.
Czesław did not want to go to summer camp, but Piotr thought differently to Czesław. The boy needed some independence and the good fresh air of the mountains and forests, he would say.
There would be new friends to meet, new activities to learn and the chance to explore in the great

outdoors.

At camp Czesław would only look forward to his father's visits at the weekend. Piotr would hire a room nearby to stay overnight and visit Czesław. When the last day of camp arrived, at long last, Czesław would have already folded and stacked all of his kit ready on the neatly made bed spread, in anticipation of Piotr arriving in the morning. Czesław could not wait to see his father, who would be on his way on the train from Warsaw, to collect him and travel back home together on the train to the city.
Czesław was stood waiting at the window, he could see his father approaching the wood chalet. It was a beautiful morning, the summer sun shone high in the blue sky, no clouds to be seen. Czesław collected his already packed bag and was out on the steps that lead to the dormitory before Piotr could get to the entrance.
"Come along Czesław, let's say goodbye to all your friends before we go" said Piotr.
 At last they were on the train travelling home. It was a couple of hours train ride back to Warsaw. Piotr had brought some treats prepared by Helena for their return trip home. The fields gave way to roads, the scenery became more urban than rural.
"Home at last" thought Czesław.

On return from summer camp Czesław was greeted by Helena and Skrawek.
Skrawek could not contain his excitement. He jumped up at Czesław and tried to remove

Czesław's eyebrows with a little pink rasping tongue.

"Look Piotr, two happy puppies together" said his adoring mother, so glad to have her little boy back home.

They both watched the spectacle, boy and dog playing happily together.

"Can I take Skrawek out for a walk?"

"But you have only just returned home" said his disappointed mother. She tried to hide the feeling of rejection in her voice. Helena had been looking forward so much to his return.

Czesław looked up with big pleading blue eyes to his mother.

"Okay, but be back in an hour. I have one of your favourite meals for you, Gołabki" said Helena.

Helena felt hurt that Czesław wanted to play out, he had been away for so long. That loving hurt between mother and child. Helena found it hard to see him growing away from her apron strings, gaining his independence, she hated the feeling of not being needed.

"Let them go and play" said Piotr gently. Piotr placed his arm around Helena, he could see the hurt in her tearful eyes and knew how she was feeling.

"Czesiek is young Helena, we have many more happy years ahead of us all, to watch this young boy grow up into a fine young man. What a great future we all have ahead of us, all together as a family."

"I could not bear to lose him, like we lost Irena" said Helena, in a quiet whisper that only Piotr

could hear.
 "I know" said Piotr, he could understand Helena's pain.

The two friends, boy and dog, ran out of the apartment doorway. Helena was there a second later with the dog lead in her hand, Czesław had forgotten the leash in his excitement to get out and play. They were already starting down the stairway. Czesław looked ahead chasing his dog, he had no thoughts of looking back.
"Slow down Skrawek" shouted Czesław.
The young dog was so excited, performing leaps and bounds along the communal grassed area in front of the blocks of the tenements. They both ran along the narrow road between the tenements that opened out and joined the main road. Czesław reached down and held Skrawek's collar.
 "Okay the road is clear, let's go."
 They both ran across the main road to the dusty track leading down to the stables, dust from the ground was kicked up behind them as they ran. Hens turned away and ran at the sight of them both bounding along followed by the cloud of dust being kicked up by paw pads and shoes. Only the cockerel stood his ground and shouted in 'Cockereleese' back at the pair bounding towards him.
Skrawek ran over to the higher mound to the right, Czesław followed. He stopped for a moment and turned to look back at the tenements from where they had come. He could just make out his mother, Helena in the distance on the balcony, she had

been watching them both. Czesław waved, his arm straight and in an exaggerated stretch so that his mother might see him. Czesław turned back towards the stables. The large brown horse came to the doorway and looked out over the split barn door. The horse nodded its head in anticipation of a treat. Czesław reached into his pocket and found a solitary mint. He held it in the flat of his hand and offered it to the horse. One sniff, a big lick and it was gone. The big rasping tongue left a wet mark on Czesław's open hand. Czesław stroked the brown long face, avoiding the snotty nose. He wiped his hand on the back of his trousers to dry off his sticky wet palm.
"Come on skrawek let's find Waldek and the others." Czesław gave the horse a final pat and turned to run back down the mound. They headed back to the main road, past the brave cockerel and scattered the hens one more time.
This time scrap did not slow down, he did not stop at the roadside, he kept on running.
There was a screech of car tyres and then a thud and a yelp.
"No Skrawek, Oh Skrawek, what's happened?" shouted Czesław.
 The car had already stopped, the driver had climbed out of the car and was walking back towards the very still little dog. Czesław could see his little friend close to the kerb. The driver bent down and gently picked up the little dog. Its head had dropped lower than its body.
 "Skrawek, oh Skrawek, is he okay?" asked Czesław to the driver, who was crouched down

next to the kerb holding the small dog in his hands. The man had a tear running down his cheek. The sight of the young boy's shock and horror and the small motionless body in his hands made him feel so helpless.

 "I'm so sorry, your dog just appeared in the road, I...I am truly sorry."

The man held out the dog to allow Czesław to stroke the little lifeless body. The dog was peaceful and still in his large hands. A small bead of blood from Skrawek's nose ran onto the fluffy white fur.

"Skrawek looks like he is asleep" said Czesław in between involuntary sobs.

"I'm so sorry, it was an accident, I could not avoid him. I feel so sad for you both. Can I give you a lift anywhere?"

"No need I live at the tenements just there."

The man gently handed over the lifeless soul to Czesław. Czesław held Skrawek to his own cheek, the little body was warm.

"Maybe he was still alive," thought Czesław.

"Maybe his little eyes will open and look up at me just like they did when I arrived home a short time ago."

Happiness can switch to sorrow in just a moment. Life is such a fragile thing.

Chapter 6

A group of neighbours, along with Czesław's family sat in their apartment sitting room around Piotr's pride and joy, his new addition to the family, a radio. A radio was not a common sight in every home. The radio had a teak polished wood finish and looked like a piece of furniture. It had two dark brown shiny Bakelite control knobs, one for the volume and on/off control and the other for a tuner knob. A large beige mesh front covered the central area where the speaker was situated. The tuner knob had to be turned to find a radio station. It was all really exciting, but today was different, no excitement, just trepidation.

The neighbours had asked to join Piotr and Helena to listen to the outcome of the meeting between the country leaders of Germany, Poland and Russia. Germany had signed a non-aggression pact with Poland back in 1934 when Hitler and the Nazi party first came into power in Germany, but this pact had been a sham. It was Hitler's clever way of preventing the possibility of a French-Polish alliance against Germany. This gave Nazi Germany the freedom and time to re-arm. Germany had been unhappy with the Treaty of Versailles following the Great War. Poland had received the former provinces of West Prussia, Poznan and Upper Silesia. Germany's discontent of the outcome of the war was the reason for Germany and Hitler's plan to start another war with Poland. The whole of Europe and Poland

were totally unprepared for this act of aggression. Neville Chamberlain, the Prime Minister of Britain, who declared "Peace for our time" was following a policy of appeasement. The objective of the policy was to maintain peace in Europe by making limited concessions to German demands. Hitler exploited this time of vulnerability in Europe, along with the knowledge that Russia was unhappy regarding their loss of land to Poland. The independence of Poland after the Great War had soured relations with Russia, due to losing control of Poland's Western borders. Russia was happy to sign a treaty with Nazi Germany at this time. Russia had no other allies in Europe. Russia was a large power that Europe held at arm's length and knew very little about. At this time there was fierce competition for economic and military dominance between Britain, France, Germany and Russia. These were volatile times in Europe.
Today the truth became apparent. It was solemn news. A serious voice was speaking on the radio situated in front of the group. Everyone stared at the box, as though they could see the newsreader. The voice was the centre of attention at this moment in time, no one in the room spoke.
"Last week on the 23rd August 1939, in Moscow, Germany and the Union of Soviet Socialist Republics signed a Treaty of Non-aggression; a neutrality pact between Nazi Germany and the Soviet Union. All talks between Germany and Poland have been exhausted. The Non-aggression pact between Nazi Germany and Poland has come to an end. On this day, the 1st of September 1939,

Poland and Germany are at war."

"Another war…no!" cried the group in the room in unison.

Germany had sited their armoured vehicles and tanks close to the Polish border weeks before the official radio announcement of war. The preparation had commenced leading up to the non-aggression treaty between Nazi Germany and Russia. The vehicles were ready to embark on the German offensive. British Embassy staff, who had already started their evacuation due to the tensions between the two countries, had reported seeing the tanks and armoured vehicles, some of which had been partly hidden by camouflage netting.

They were there in large numbers ready and waiting at the Western border.

Within the hour of the radio announcement, bomber planes were heard over Warsaw. The Polish army and Air Force fought bravely. They had only limited resources, 500 tanks, one million soldiers and 400 aircraft, against 13 million German soldiers, 2500 tanks and 2000 aircraft. Germany had been building up their armament along with soldier and air force personnel numbers ever since their defeat following World War I. This was done surreptitiously in violation of the Treaty of Versailles, held in 1919. Glider clubs were used to train pilots and sporting clubs to train soldiers to shoot. When Adolf Hitler along with his Nazi party came to power in Germany in 1933, he openly spoke out about the German rearmament. Within 17 months of him announcing the rearmament programme, the Army, made up of volunteers and conscripts, reached its projected forecast of 36 divisions. Before his election, Hitler and his Nazi party had been openly campaigning to take back land that Germany had lost after the Great War.

Germany claimed it was a defensive action. Hitler wanted to gain space for the expanding population of Germany. The long time plan was coming in to action. This was going to be the second of World Wars in Piotr's lifetime. Piotr had fought in the first Great War, only 21 years previously. The adults in the room still had fresh memories of the Great War. Only days later after the German attack on Poland, the Soviet army took its opportunity to regain territory from Poland. Russia struck from the East, invading Poland on September 17th 1939. Poland was now annexed between the two invaders. Despite attacks on all fronts, the Polish army continued the battle for 35 days. Warsaw was overrun on the 28th of September, pockets of resistance continued the fight in other cities. This defiance by the outnumbered Polish army gave Britain and its allies time to prepare for the inevitable war. To avoid loss of civilian life, the Polish troops were pulled out of Poland to France and neutral Romania. Barbara, Helena's sister, told Helena that her own brother Stanley was leaving Poland, with the other Polish military personnel to regroup with the Allies to form an attack from outside of the country. The Russian and German forces would have annihilated the poorly equipped troops if they had continued a defense from within their own homeland. Czesław's half-brother

Władysław was part of the Polish resistance. Władysław looked very much like Czesław's half-sister Irena, he had the dark thick hair and was fearless just like Irena had been. He was 17 years older than Czesław. When he saw his little brother Czesław, he always made a big fuss of him.
The resistance bravely assisted the movement and regrouping of Polish soldiers, sailors and aircrew to take on the fight from outside Poland.
Stanley joined an all Polish naval crew on the ship Piorun, *Lightning bolt* in English. Piorun was an N class destroyer built on the River Clyde, in Glasgow, Scotland. The ship was commissioned by the British Royal Navy and given over as a replacement of the Polish ORP Grom, a destroyer which had been torpedoed off the Norwegian coast on 4 May 1940.
Czesław was only 13 at the outbreak of the war.

Chapter 7

"I'm off to the cinema tonight" announced an excited Czesław,

"Czesiek you have school work to complete. You have exams soon, you know if you get good results you will be able to join the apprentice scheme where I work at the Telegraph office as an engineer" replied Piotr. His voice could be heard from the kitchen.

"But Father, there is a lovely film on at the cinema and all my friends are going."

"Czesiek, your school work comes first."

Czesław knew, like Poland, he would not win this battle, so he retreated to his bedroom.

The following day Czesław went to school. He had been thinking about his friends who had been at the cinema, while he was doing his studies. What a wonderful time they must have had together. Czesław knew they would be all too ready to tell him what a great time they had and all about the fantastic film. He was not looking forward to the banter and giggles at his expense.

Czesław with friends in Warsaw, age 17.
The winter before his incarceration

"My parents can be such a pain, spoiling my fun" thought Czesław.

He walked along the school corridors expecting to see his friends, but they were nowhere to be seen. A couple of his class mates were consoling one of the girls from his class, who was sobbing uncontrollably. He immediately recognised that feeling of grief, from when he had lost his beautiful sister Irena.

"Kristina what's wrong? What's happened?" Something was wrong. Something was very wrong.

"No, this can't be happening, this cannot be true" he thought to himself. The horror hit him as though he had been dealt a physical blow to his body.

The pupils were all told to gather in the main hall for their morning assembly. Czesław's stomach was tightening in a knot, he was confused. This could not be real. The headmaster stood in front of the gathered children in the school assembly. He spoke calmly to the silent group.

"Four of our dearly valued pupils were shot last night by German soldiers, as a lesson for the previous actions of the Resistance. It was in retaliation to the fact that a German soldier had been killed. As a lesson to the people of Warsaw, everyone in the cinema was rounded up and ordered to go outside. The entire group from the cinema were...killed by a firing squad. Let us pray for the souls of our departed friends."

That could have been me last night, thought Czesław. I would have been number five.

Chapter 8

Czesław followed in his father's footsteps, as did many school leavers, all following their parents' careers in the pre-internet world.
Czesław joined the Post and Telegraph office in Warsaw where his father also worked. He joined as an apprentice engineer working on Morse code communications.

Czesław loved the companionship of his friends. He kept in contact with his friends from the younger days. The days when they all played football out on the green in front of the flats. His skating girlfriends were growing up too, Czesław remembered teasing them and pulling their pony tails.
"Pałac Wilanowie this weekend" said Czesław. Wilanów Palace or Wilowski Palace, as it is also known, is a royal baroque palace residence located in the Wilanów district of Warsaw in a large park area. It was a popular meeting spot.
"Okay, I'll be there" said Waldek.
"I'll bring the harmonica," said Czesław "Jurek has said he will bring the piano accordion"
"Rather him than me," scoffed Waldek "that instrument is a monster to carry, I'll bring my guitar."
The group met at the tram stop early that Sunday morning. There was a large gathering of people waiting for the tram. The boys joined the group and one by one started to play their instruments.

Czesław started it off with his harmonica. It was a familiar old tune and the group of people all knew the words to the song. In wartime, moments like these were precious. Couples held each other, some listened some sang along with the young musicians.
"Today's a great day to be alive" smiled Czesław, looking around at the singing crowd.
The music continued on the tram, Waldek's hat was being filled with money from the happy passengers.
Most of the day was spent under the shade of a large tree with a picnic, more music and of course friendship.

The weekend passed all too quickly. Monday at work went along as Mondays do. Working in the same building, Czesław met Waldek on the way home. They both walked along the City footpaths chatting about the events of the day, the streets were busy with people leaving their places of work. The air was a milder and dryer air now than in the previous winter months. The warm sunlight hung low in the ever extending day light of spring. Food was in short supply since the occupation. Czesław and Waldek were talking about a plan to get meat and eggs for their families.
"The queues are getting longer every day at the shops" whispered Czesław.
"Yes, my mum is up at four in the morning queuing for food" said Waldek in agreement.
"There is a way we can help our parents" started Czesław, as he looked around to make sure no one

was listening.
A man had stopped near them to tie his shoelace. The two friends stopped talking and waited for the old boy to tie the knot and move on, before they continued with their covert conversation. Left over right, right over left and the same again, this was going to take a while…
"Look, I know where we can get some homemade alcohol. My brother can help us, he can put me in touch with a supplier."
Waldek's jaw dropped open in disbelief. He had never seen Czesław so serious.
"The war is certainly changing you Czesław."
"What?" said Czesław, his own words had even shocked himself, "We have to do something you know."
"I don't know…" replied Waldek. "These are dangerous times."
Nothing more was said as they set off to walk again.
The sound of gunshots rang out. The boys ran and pressed up against a wall, not knowing what to expect. A tram nearby carrying weary workers home was being ordered to stop. Soldiers stood on the track, weapons raised and pointing at the tram to stop its progress. The driver was desperately trying to slow down the heavily laden tram, the sound of metal wheels sliding on metal tracks added to the drama. The tram came to an intense sliding stop. The soldiers were angry. They shouted loudly, causing confusion and fear amongst the people on the tram. The enraged voices shouted loudly in German; they were

ordering the passengers to leave the stationary tram. People nearby, just like Czesław and Waldek, watched the spectacle unfold. A child started to cry, no other sound could be heard now. There was an eerie silence that hung over the scene, the normal to and fro of people and traffic was at a halt.

People stopped and watched in disbelief, disconnected from the scene unfolding in front of them. It was almost like watching a film at the local cinema, the scene alien and unreal. One soldier broke the silence and shouted "RAUSE, RAUSE…" The people from the tram were shepherded to stand in front of a high wall just metres from where Czesław and Waldek stood.

"These people…" a voice shouted in perfect Polish, "Your people, are going to be punished for crimes committed by others against the German occupying forces. A soldier has been killed by your own Polish Resistance Army. These people are friends and relations of yours, they are nothing but saboteurs. Their defiance will not be tolerated by your German occupying forces. For every soldier that your saboteurs kill, we will execute 50 of your people; your family, friends, citizens of Warsaw. You will be rounded up and punished for these crimes. You will all witness this today."

A soldier moved towards a tall wooden door that was the entrance to the City Hall. He nailed a list to the door.

"You must all go and read this list of names. The names included in the list will be the next 50 people to be executed. You all must learn that if you do not listen to our words, your families will pay for the consequences."

Soldiers surrounded the group of people that had been herded to the wall. On command from the soldier making the speech, the soldiers lifted their rifles.

"Take aim!"

The voyeurs moved back slowly in silence, even the birds did not sing anymore. All the traffic on the normally busy street was at a standstill. It was so silent.

"No this is a mistake, you cannot do this," a brave man's voice protested from the audience. The soldier, Mr. Speaker, looked around to catch the eye of the defiant person who was interrupting his show. It was the very man that had been tying his shoe lace next to Czesław and Waldek earlier.

"It's Mr. Shoelace" Czesław whispered to Waldek.

"You!" growled Mr. Speaker. He was angry with the defiant observer, "Him!"

A soldier pushed into the crowd and pulled the old guy forward, as he protested his innocence. Czesław had learnt quickly not to make eye contact or speak when being in the presence of anyone like these soldiers. The old guy was taken to join the people stood with their backs to the wall.

"You!" shouted Mr. Speaker, pointing to a young girl silently sobbing. Her shoulders were rising and falling in an involuntary action, caused by her silent sobs. She was only in her teens, about Czesław's age, 17 maybe.

"You! Move forward, leave the condemned group.

Come, you are saved by this foolish old man."
The execution squad of soldiers, relaxed and pointed their rifles down to the ground.
"Now I have too many to teach the lesson to. I only need 50 lives today. You are a very lucky young girl."
The girl did not want to move. She was stood with an older couple, about the older guy's age. The woman next to her looked like an older version of the young girl. She spoke to the young girl, begging her to go, "Go…go!" She shooed her daughter away for her own good, the natural protective mother's instinct was to protect her child.
Mr. Speaker did not need to speak loudly to be heard, the silence was so intense. There wasn't a sound from the crowd.
"Now young lady turn and watch. You will watch!" The veins on Mr. Speaker's neck stood proud with the exertion of his voice.
Mr. Speaker repeated himself again, just in case anyone had forgotten his chilling speech.
"For every soldier killed, we will take back 50 lives."
The young girl's shoulders started to move up and down again, she was now sobbing uncontrollably. Her mother began to breakdown too, she had tried to stay strong for her daughter. Her daughter was now safe. She turned to the man next to her.
"But who will look after our daughter now, maybe my sister will look after her?" She herself had no time to ask her sister for this assistance. The man supported her with his arm around her, as he

pulled a handkerchief from his pocket on the front of his jacket. He would never have thought when he put on his jacket that very morning and placed an ironed handkerchief in the breast pocket of his jacket that he would actually need the handkerchief. He gently, lovingly dried his partner's eyes. Maybe more so to shield his love's eyes from what was about to happen to them. He had himself seen killing on the frontline during the First World War. He had expected every day that he would be killed in the battle. He never imagined that his life was going to end on the streets of the City of Warsaw. He had survived the trenches, he had killed German soldiers with his bare hands when he had run out of bullets. He had listened to their screams, but that was in the battlefield, soldier against soldier, each soldier killing or be killed. Today was different, he had no weapon, he had no hate for Mr. Speaker and his adrenalin was not flowing.

He felt a great sorrow for his wife and their beautiful daughter that they were both leaving behind. Both were the love of his life, his reason to exist. He was no longer able to protect them from danger, he would never see his daughter progress through life. Who would she marry? Would she have her own children? This was the end for him and his lifelong partner. The young sobbing girl stretched her arms out as if to touch the fingers of her mother's outstretched arms, they held each other's wild gaze…

"Take aim!" Mr. Speaker ordered.

The rifles lifted for a second time. One soldier

visibly trembled, the barrel of his weapon was rising and falling as he tried to calm himself down to take aim. The soldier looked a similar age to the girl that had been rescued. Mr. Shoelace did not move, he had accepted his fate. His own life in exchange for another, a young girl who had all her life ahead of her…

"FIRE!"

The noise was louder than any noise that Czesław had ever heard before. Screams sounded from the onlookers. The victims fell and lay silent.

Mr. Speaker walked forward, his Astra 600 handgun at the ready, its barrel reflecting the evening sun. He was going to finish the job, just like a vet putting a horse out of its misery.

Shots sounded from Mr. Speaker's gun, his targets twitched at the report from his handgun.

He summoned other soldiers over to finish the job. He could not be bothered to reload his own weapon.

The smell of cordite hung in the air, like at a firework spectacular in the park, but there was no feeling of excitement at this event. Another smell permeated the air, like the smell you are greeted with in a butcher's shop, where raw meat is hung.

The sobbing girl fell to her knees, she was all alone in her grief.

Czesław was violently sick against the wall that they had pressed themselves against. He could taste the acidic bile from his vomit in his mouth.

The boys turned and ran from the scene, the images of the scene replaying in their minds. There was no way to make the images stop.

Nothing was said between the two boys on the way home. At the tenement flats, Waldek turned and said "I'm in. I'll do the food run with you Czes." Czesław nodded, nothing more was said.
The following Friday Czesław and Waldek went to their office managers and asked for an Ausweis, Werkausweis, Personenausweis, identification documents related to the place of employment. During the occupation such documents allowed the bearer to travel outside of the City. There was less chance of detention if you had the documents. Larger companies, such as the Post Office that employed Czesław, had records of all their employees, this gave them the authority to issue the cards.

Chapter 9

Czesław met with his brother Władysław. His brother was part of the Resistance, this was the largest underground resistance movement in Europe. The Polish resistance was the Polish Home Army, whose allegiance was to the Polish government-in-exile in France and later in London. It was used to disrupt supplies to the Eastern front, provided military intelligence to the British and saved many Jewish lives. They successfully helped many of the Polish forces to escape to fight from outside of Poland.

Czesław went to collect the home distilled alcohol. It would be used as a currency. A Stolichnaya style Russian alcohol is a vodka made of wheat and rye grain, the resulting liquid is distilled three times to a strength of 96.4% alcohol by volume.
"What's with the canvas sacks and flour?" asked Czesław.
"Those sacks Czesiek, are for carrying the flasks of vodka hidden in the flour. On return from the farm, hide the hams and eggs within the flour. If you are questioned, deny all knowledge of the sacks, make sure you place them in the overhead racks of the train compartment well away from where you are sitting. You must be careful, this is serious stuff you are getting into Czesiek. This is not a game. If anything goes wrong, leave the goodies and get away, do you understand? If they catch you, they will take you away to the

Concentration camps."

"Camps?" asked Czesław
 "Do you know the Germans have built large detention centres where they are taking people? Any excuse is good enough to take people away...the detained are never seen by their loved ones ever again!"
Czesław was not listening to the scary bits, he was more interested in the sacks; this was a finger in the eye to the Germans. Czesław felt no remorse, the gunshots and the blood on the streets were still replaying in his mind like an endless nightmare and it was even worse when he closed his eyes. The images would not go away, they would never go away. This act would be a small victory for Czesław against the occupiers of Poland and would be a great needed food supply for his family. His mother was up at four every morning to join the queues outside the shops. Everyone in the queue was hopeful they would get something nice to take home to feed their families.

The birds had started their morning song, the early sunlight was piercing through the gap in Czesław's bedroom curtains. He had not slept all night long. He had been rehearsing in his mind, placing the sacks and sitting well away from the goodies. "No sir that's not mine...."
The smell of boiling porridge now permeated into Czesław's bedroom. Piotr had got up early to cook up a warm sendoff breakfast for his son.

Piotr was tired, he also had not slept. Helena had spent most of the night waking and asking Piotr to change their son's mind.
 "He should not risk his life on this new venture." Piotr had reassured Helena, "Czesiek can look after himself, he is now 17."
Although in his mind Piotr was not as confident as he sounded, Piotr was worried also.
"Boys grow up quickly in wartime" said Piotr, remembering his time as a soldier in the First World War.

"Morning Father" said a bleary eyed Czesław.
"You look tired Czesiek are you Okay?"
"Fine Father, I'll be all the better after a bowl of your best porridge."
"Good man Czesiek, sit down I'll serve you some, it's all ready for you."
"Bacon for breakfast tomorrow Father, you wait and see!"
"Czesiek, stay at home. You don't need to go today" said a tired looking Helena. She had entered the room silently, her eyes were red and swollen through lack of sleep and tears.
Czesław went over to his mother, she appeared so vulnerable today. Czesław had never seen this in her before, she was always strong and reassuring. Today the roles had reversed, Czesław was the one who tried to make his mother feel better.
"By tonight, we will have food in the larder. We will all feel better with food in our bellies." said Czesław.
All three stood together in a huddle. Helena's

recover some of the food from the wreckage. Only one of the soldiers appeared to have survived. He was not like any other soldier we knew. Not SS, he did not have the SS runes on his tunic. Possibly in his 50s. He came towards us and held his hands palms down directing them at us, his audience, as if he was fanning the flames of an imaginary fire. He was doing the old calm down, calm down mime. There was a murmur among the camp prisoners as he spoke. I got closer to listen.
"I know you are all deeply disappointed about what has become of your food. Yes, you must hate the pilots that destroyed our convoy and all the food that we were transporting to you. This food was sent for you all to eat, there was an enormous amount of food, enough for you all. But, listen to me, this food was no good. All the food was contaminated, it had been poisoned. It was being sent to you, to finish you all off." His hand pointed to us all in a large sweeping gesture.
The crowd slowly started to take in the information that had just been given by the soldier who stood in front of us, in a German soldier's uniform. Could we trust this information? Could we believe him? Some of the crowd still shouted at the soldier in anger.
"Don't shoot the messenger" he said, "I am a simple soldier, I do not have an SS badge, like the soldiers that guarded you in your camps."
He held his jacket lapel in his left hand to demonstrate. We could see his badly burnt hand caused by the aerial bombardment he ragged his lapel backwards and forwards with his injured

hand, for us all to see that he did not have the Schtzstaffel Runes on his lapel.

"The decisions were not mine. But let me say your allies did you the biggest favour ever."

He pointed up in to the sky where the screaming engines of the planes had been.

"They have prolonged your lives." he shouted.

Prolonged was the perfect term in war. We were lucky this time but there could be many more encounters with the Grim Reaper anytime soon. There was a stir among the prisoners, those that had stood up to protest sat back down, partly out of agreement and mostly out of fatigue, exasperated by starvation.

The soldier could see the anger of the group slowly subside. We were prisoners that were beaten into submission at the slightest remonstration against a German uniform. He knew that if he stood up straight and barked his instruction he could get through to the mob. He was a shy, quiet man, he was not used to instructing large groups of murderous prisoners. His will to fight had long gone.

"Today you can rest, tomorrow we will leave this evil place, this death camp" he told us.

The remaining SS soldiers were nowhere to be seen. After they had witnessed the attack on the convoy and it's destruction, they knew their mission was over. They had hoped most of the malnourished prisoners would have died on the death march. The food was just a back-up plan, in case some hardy individuals survived.

"Tomorrow we will leave and move towards your

shoulders rose and fell with each sob.

The railway platform was quite full. Czesław was pleased, as this would help the two of them to stay anonymous and hidden amongst a crowd. No one needed to use the old stone building waiting room as a shelter today, it stood empty at the side of the platform. The sun was bright in its ascendance, there were some very high wispy clouds in the pinky blue sky and the ground was starting to dry under the sun's rays. The air smelt fresher in the morning. Czesław liked the freshness that the early morning brought with it.
"Play your harmonica Czesław, let's get everyone singing." said Waldek. He was always the life and soul of the party. Czesław could feel Waldek's inner strength transferring across to him. Positive friends always made Czesław feel good, just like the feeling of this morning's sun on his face.
There was no need to reply, Waldek would be quipping all day long.
The crowd moved forward together. Czesław could not see the train yet. He stood up from his temporary seat clutching his sacks, as when in a crowd you instinctively move with it, it must be the herd instinct inside us all.
"It's here then" said Waldek.
"Seems that way" replied Czesław.
With much pushing and squeezing, the crowd dissolved through the carriage doors like shoaling fish entering a submerged shipwreck.
"Sacks up here, us over there" motioned Czesław, looking around for seats further down the carriage.

They found a pair of empty seats, from where they could easily see the sacks. It was not so much the feeling that the sacks would be stolen, more the preparation for denial of all knowledge if the sacks were seized by the German soldiers.
"Let's get some sleep, it's going to be about an hour until we get to Tłuszcz." advised Waldek.
"Yes, as if I could sleep now" Czesław answered.
"Suit yourself Czesław, I'll get some shut eye for both of us."
The train rocked gently, with the rhythmic sound of the wheels passing over the tracks joints.
They passed over the Vistula River, German armoured cars protected the bridge entrances at both sides of the riverbank. The mist over the fields was starting to burn off in the sunlight as they entered Legionowo. This was the halfway point of their journey.
Some passengers left the train and were replaced by more people who took their seats. The sacks remained in their place in the overheads.
Czesław's eyelids were starting to feel heavy as the closing doors clattered in preparation for its departure from Legionowo. A burst on the engine whistle sounded in a shrill extended *peeeeep* and the steam engine blew smoke from its chimney. The strain was taken up on the carriages, which jolted and hardly moved, as would a line of reluctant children being pulled along by their parent, who then followed along obediently, clickity clacking over the tracks.
"Tickets, Ausweis, papers."
A German soldier was following the ticket

collector. The soldier must have been bored and thought he would upset the locals by checking their papers.

Czesław was woken by the sound of the request. What, no, it's not mine, where are my papers...Czesław regained his senses, hoping no one could hear the thoughts screaming in his head. On the outside he appeared to be calmly reaching into his pocket to pull out his papers. These were his permission to travel papers, they had been issued by the Warsaw Post Office where he worked. The soldier and ticket collector briefly looked at the tickets and papers and passed by. Czesław's heart was racing as though he had been running for the train, the fight or flight response had kicked in; the surge of adrenalin raced around his body, it was preparing him to react to a threat to his life. He had read about this in his biology classes at school, hardly taking it in at the time, instead thinking about skating in the park with his friends or playing football near the tenements. Everything felt so safe, so predictable in those days, now that secure feeling was gone. Czesław had never felt safe again since the massacre he had witnessed on the streets of Warsaw, on his way back from work that fateful evening. The good, content feeling that had been inside him as he walked home after a day at work had been crushed as he witnessed the lives of fellow citizens being extinguished in front of him. He had never seen a dead person before that day. The image of carnage had triggered flash backs, night sweats. No one knew what post-traumatic stress disorder was at that time, now a recognised condition; a disorder caused by very stressful, frightening or distressing events. Czesław did not know why he felt as he did, he could not discuss it with anyone except his father. His father had been a soldier and still suffered from the flashbacks of the battles himself. He told Czesław about how he had lost his finger when a grenade had exploded and how he had laid bleeding from his hand. He had felt a shockwave of air that lifted him off his feet and flung him to the floor, as if he was a rag doll. The force had hit his ears and made all sound remote and distorted, the air pressure had been like a gale force blast of sharp grit-filled wind. No pain at first, no sound other than ringing in his ears. He had lain down after the blast, stunned and defenseless like being immersed in a dream when you try to run in your sleep, but cannot move in your nightmare. His friends lay around him, some screaming, some deadly still. Jan lay still to his right looking at him, his mouth was moving, but Piotr could not hear any sound. Piotr felt like his head was submerged underwater, he could only hear muffled noises. He crawled over to Jan as close as he could and lay next to him. Piotr put his ear to Jan's mouth. He could hear gurgling as blood ran out of his comrade's mouth. His lifelong friend tried to speak, but his lungs had been destroyed by the blast, he could no longer project sound. Piotr tried to turn Jan over but could not grasp him. Only then did he realise that he had lost part of his little finger. Jan lay motionless.

"At least he had not died alone" Piotr had told

Czesław "I had been there with him, to the end."
Piotr had continued the battle even though he was wounded. A canister in his tunic had stopped shrapnel entering his chest cavity.
"I would have suffered the same fate as Jan if the shrapnel had pierced my vital organs." explained Piotr.
Piotr was taken from the frontline to the temporary support hospital, where he had his wounds cleaned and dressed. After a couple of days he grew stronger.
"This was in your torn and bloodied jacket pocket" said the nurse, handing a fob watch to Piotr.
"It looks like a German watch" said the nurse.
"Yes, I found it laid in the mud when we overran the German trenches…Ha at least now I will know what time it is when I make my return to the frontline" jested Piotr to the nurse.

Signs for Tłuszcz appeared on the platform outside. People began to gather their belongings, Czesław and Waldek walked towards the sacks. They felt that everyone's eyes were on them, yet in reality everyone was too busy going about their own business. No doubt some of the other passengers had their own guilty secrets hidden in their bags too.
The farm was about twenty minutes' walk from the station. They started their walk, leaving the hustle and bustle of the station behind them.
"How do you know, where to go and who to ask for?" asked Waldek.
"Easy" replied Czesław, "I'm looking for a

Smugglers This Way sign…ha, come on keep up Waldemar" joked Czesław, using Waldek's full name to wind him up.

Czesław's brother had told him the route from the station and he was remembering the instructions in his mind. Nothing could be written down, as it was all very top secret.

Czesław felt his confidence returning for the first time since leaving home.

They had left the main road and were now walking up a narrow lane with fences and bushes either side.

"These bags are heavy" panted Waldek.

The sacks containing the bottles and flour were made of rough sacking and were cutting into their hands.

"Look there, I'm going to ask the farm lady" said Czesław.

"Hi, is your husband here? I have some business for him" said Czesław, trying to keep his voice low and deep so that he sounded older than his years. Czesław thought that if he sounded older he may be taken more seriously.

"What kind of business?" asked the red knuckled rosy cheeked middle-aged lady, breaking off from hanging out a pair of large long johns. If they were the farmers Czesław was looking for and if things went wrong, Czesław would have no trouble running away, it would be like outrunning Humpty Dumpty.

"I have some sacks for him." explained Czesław.

The rosy cheeked lady's attention was fully grasped at these words. She rubbed her red chapped hands on her blue checked apron, an apron that was not as clean as his mother's apron thought Czesław.

"Wait right there" ordered the farmer's wife.

She marched off towards the shed, where metal hammering on metal came from.

Children's red cheeked and rounded faces appeared at the farmhouse lounge window.

"They must be the farmers' children, they look just like her" Czesław thought to himself.

"Is this all going to plan? " asked Waldek, sat on a wall, legs swinging as if he was back in the park playground waiting for his friends to arrive and play football.

"Not sure yet" replied Czesław, his eyes still fixed on the farmhouse. Its stone slates had moss growing on the north facing roof. You didn't see roof moss in the city, the air was not as pure as in the countryside. The acidity of the sulphur pollution emitted from the factories killed off the moss on the city buildings' rooftops, but not out here in the sticks.

"What kind of goodies you got here boys?" questioned a red faced, red headed, large man with a balding pate. The farmer reminded Czesław of Friar Tuck in the tales of Robin Hood.

"Liquid business sir" replied Czesław.

"You had better bring that to the barn then boys." Friar Tuck eagerly grabbed a couple of sacks from Czesław like an excited child anticipating a Christmas present.

"Looks like you said the right things Czesław" smiled Waldek, following behind with a sack over each shoulder.

They entered the subdued light in the barn and Czesław's eyes widened as he took in the array of hams and salami hung from the rafters. A big hammer lay on the workbench, along with a stack of nails that Friar Tuck must have been using to hang up the hams. They had heard the hammering as they approached the farm. Czesław involuntarily wretched at the smell of the freshly slaughtered hams. His flashbacks to the carnage on the city streets ran through his mind again, triggered by the smell of blood in the barn.

"You okay boy?" frowned Friar Tuck, looking a little concerned at Czesław's pale and sweating face.

"Yes fine just a bit travel sick" replied Czesław.

"Get some glasses Ivanna, let's try out the goodies" said Friar Tuck.

Ivanna disappeared out of the barn towards the farmhouse, at a speed that indicated there must have been a drought recently at Tuck's house. She returned with four glasses.

"Looks like it's going to be a party" thought Czesław.

Friar Tuck reached into one of the sacks. He felt for the hard smooth surface of a flask. He pulled it out and held it high, brushing off the remaining flour, a movement that rather resembled as if he had just delivered a young calf. He was looking at the flask for clarity, holding it up towards the light entering the barn entrance. Friar Tuck gave a low growl in his throat like an old pirate, Czesław hoped this was a sign of approval. Friar Tuck filled

all four glasses.
"Drink" demanded Friar Tuck, nodding at each boy in turn, probably checking if they had brought him a bottle of poison.
"I think that's an order not a request Czes, I don't think our host trusts us fully yet." said Waldek.
"Ahh OK, Na zdrowie!" said Czesław, lifting the glass high.
Czesław pinched his nose and took the shot. Waldek did the same. The boys swallowed and then gasped for breath as though a fire monster had entered their throats and was now heading up their noses and down in to their lungs. After what seemed a lifetime, their wind passages relaxed and allowed them to suck in the air they desperately required.
Friar Tuck and his wife chinked glasses together and laughed at the choking boys and replied
 "Na zdrowie."
The liquid disappeared down their throats as easy as if they were drinking a glass of their best creamy milk.
 "Good" grunted Friar Tuck.
"Looks like you've passed the test Czes" whispered Waldek, who was still gasping air as though he had been pearl diving.
The boys received in return their sacks, still full of flour, with added hams, eggs and salami hidden within them. If anyone challenged them, they would say they were taking bags of flour home for their family. Hopefully no German soldier would volunteer to risk getting their smart uniforms covered in flour, by searching inside the sacks.

Back at the tenement blocks, the boys gave each other a large hand shake and hugs of relief after their adventure together.
"See you tomorrow evening Waldek. We will eat like kings tonight" grinned Czesław.
Helena greeted Czesław like a proud mother penguin greeting and fussing over her young chick.
 "Tell me what happened, are you okay? Did you find your way, was it difficult, what happened?" questioned Helena, without even taking a single breath.

"One question at a time Mama" said a very proud Czesław" feeling like the great provider for the family.
Czesław rolled up his sleeves before he dug his hands into the first flour sack. Triumphantly he pulled out a large ham shoulder followed by smoked kiełbasa, Kabonos, Wiejska, large brown and white eggs. His arms were covered in the flour and Czesław started to laugh out loud. He had forgotten the feeling of happiness; it was so comforting to feel happiness returning to him.
Helena moved across to Czesław and hugged her son with a squeeze that only mothers can do, as she squeezed the air from Czesław's lungs. Helena began to laugh with her son.
Piotr brushed away a tear that trickled down his cheek, he had not seen his family so happy for a long time. Everything had changed since the time they had sat together in the lounge listening to the

news on the radio. Listening to the announcement that the German's were at the borders ready to invade their country.
Piotr was so proud of him, his boy was growing in to a man. The War had changed his son, he was becoming strong, the way he remembered his friends change in the previous war.
People become very close and appreciated much simpler things, like love, family and of course a full stomach.
This supply of food would last them a month. Piotr felt content and more secure. Maybe they would survive this turmoil together after all. They all could feel their strong family bond.

"It's been a month Waldek. We need to get ourselves ready for another trip to Tłuszcz" said Czesław.

It was an early start, they had a mission to complete. It was cold, the sun was still low, hidden behind the tenement blocks and everything looked monochrome in the long shadows. The air smelt sweet, even in the city, the fresh cold morning air. The birds had already started their morning symphony. Muscles were tight in their bodies. That feeling of needing to stretch due to their bodies' inactivity through sleep was overpowering.
"This was way too early in the morning for a weekend" thought Czesław.
"Ausweis?" asked Czesław.
"Yes!" mumbled Waldek. He was not a morning person.

The train was full. Some people were standing. The goodies had been stashed in their usual place, on the overhead racks. Some people were looking out of the windows, some chatting. Czesław turned from his seat to look down the aisle, he could just about see around the people stood up in the aisle. Through the partition door window he could see the shoulder of a soldier in uniform, in fact it looked like a carriage full of German soldiers. There was a sea of grey uniforms in the adjoining carriage.
"Looks like we have company today" said Czesław.
There was no reply from a sleepy Waldek.
His head had fallen back and his mouth was wide open. Czesław looked at Waldek and thought that is what Waldek would look like dead.
Through the carriage window, fields had replaced houses, the sun was rising, the clickety-clacking was smooth and rhythmic, Czesław's eyes grew heavy and started to close. Czesław drifted into a recurring dream. A familiar crowd stood in front of him, hands outstretched begging for his help. A girl stood looking down at two people, they were her parents. Their eyes were closed, tears ran from under their closed eyelids, their bodies were lifeless on the ground…
"Stop him! He will kill us all!"
Czesław woke to a frenzy of shouting and the strong smell of fuel vapour.
A man was stood up from his seat, rocking his body forwards and backwards, his baggy brown trousers and dark green jumper were wet, as was

his hair, wet. He was pouring a liquid from a can that he held up above his head. He chanted "Kill the Germans, we are all going to die!" over and over again.

People tried to make some distance between the man and them, which was not easy in the crowded carriage. This was bad news for Czesław and Waldek. With their cargo of alcohol and carriages full of German soldiers being transported on the same train, this was not going to be a good day out.

Czesław stood and grabbed his friend by the coat sleeve, dragging him from his seat and up onto his feet. Czesław did not know what he was going to do once they were stood up, but he knew they needed to move, now and as quick as possible. Czesław looked around the carriage, all eyes were on the fuel soaked man. The man's hair was now on fire. Czesław pushed through the line of screaming passengers, squeezed through the sea of panic stricken bodies and managed to get them both to the carriage door. He looked up at the cord that was horizontal above the door. He had always wanted to pull that stop cord. He had always wondered what would happen. He reached up and grabbed the line. He read the sign over and over as he had done so many times before and pulled with all his might on the cord. *'ONLY PULL THIS CORD IN THE EVENT OF AN EMERGENCY'*
Forget the 100 Zloty fine for pulling the cord, they needed to escape.

They lurched forward as the rope had done its job and almost instantly, there was a screeching of

metal on metal, the train had started to slow. Czesław pushed down the window of the carriage doorway and reached outside for the big handle on the door. The ground outside was still moving quickly; it looked a long way down without a platform below them. Czesław pushed with his shoulder as he turned the handle. With his other hand he kept hold of his friend's coat sleeve. He squeezed the sleeve to make sure there was still an arm in the jacket, he didn't want to leave the train with a jacket and no Waldek. Czesław looked into the carriage, he could now feel the heat from the burning body, seats either side of him had set alight. The man was now in a kneeling position, the flames rising a metre above his head. People were throwing coats over him as the German soldiers began to appear from the other carriage. If the alcohol within the sacks ignited things would get even worse.
"Let's go!" ordered Czesław.
"It's still moving!" protested Waldek.
"Now!" shouted Czesław, to make himself heard through the noise of panic within the carriage. The pair of them were now in midair outside of the carriage, both held their breath at the same moment in time and waited for the impact as gravity took control of their bodies. Both hit the dry ground and they hit it hard. They tumbled along the rough uneven ground, surrounded by a dust cloud, air was forced from their lungs on impact with the unforgiving ground.
Their ears rang and stars flashed in their tightly closed eyes. For a moment they lay motionless,

stunned by the battering. Slowly as if in slow-motion, they sat up together.
Waldek had a great big smile on his face. "Again, again!"
"Come on let's get away from here!" exclaimed a breathless Czesław.
"No bones broken, I don't think" said Waldek.
 The adrenalin kicked in, no pain registered.
Czesław looked around, "There!"
A train was approaching from Tłuszcz. Czesław pushed then pulled Janek, who had frozen like a rabbit in an oncoming headlight beam.
 "Go!" instructed Czesław.
Their legs slowly started to respond, following their sensory overload of excitement, fear and pain. If they got this wrong they would both be dead. No doubt about it, they would be seen as saboteurs, their alcohol adding to the fuel and combustion. They scrambled up to the railway track on their elbows, keeping low under the carriages. They lay motionless and waited until the train passed on the opposite track. It slowed near the station platform. It was pure luck that they were near a station. They both stood up and aimed to run around the rear of the Warsaw-bound train. They heaved themselves off the track onto the high platform. As the last of the passengers entered the train, they ran to the carriage doors and jumped straight into the arms of a German soldier.
Czesław stiffened as the soldiers welcomed them both aboard.
"Move up" said the soldier to his fellow soldiers.
Two soldiers moved aside to let the two dusty boys

move into the carriage. Most of the passengers were looking across at the burning wreckage at the other side of the track. Smoke bellowed out of one of the carriages. Two small explosions erupted and could be seen and heard by the onlookers.

"What's happening here? Did you see from the platform?" the soldier asked the two boys.

"Looks like a fire on other train..." Czesław replied, shrugging his shoulders for effect.

They both moved down the carriage to join the other passengers. They were all looking out of the window at the spectacle. Soldiers from the burning train were already out on the platform, rounding up the passengers into a large group. The soldiers were pushing the younger passengers into a smaller group.

"They will be going to the camps" said Czesław under his breath, "My brother told me about the camps."

Chapter 10

"I was thinking of doing another goodie run" said Czesław to his brother Władysław.
"Times are getting more difficult Czesław, the Germans are rounding up more and more people for hardly any reason. You would be taken away for sure if you were caught with the vodka or on your return journey with the food."
"The flour bags would hide the goodies" said Czesław, distracted by what he could see and hear going on outside Władysław's flat.
Shots could be heard outside. A woman screamed. Czesław went through the doorway and out onto the balcony; he could see over the ghetto wall from there.
"There are fires…buildings are on fire! They are fighting, what's happening?" exclaimed Czesław.
The Polish Jews and the Romany people had been rounded up within days of the German invasion and forced to live in enclosed ghettos. The Warsaw ghetto had a population of 200,000 people per square mile. They were living in terrible, cramped conditions. Unemployment was a major problem in the ghettos, because no employment meant no money for food and essentials. Workshops were created to manufacture goods to be sold illegally to the world outside the confines of the ghetto. Raw goods were purchased and smuggled into the

enclosure. The buying and selling was often the task of the children. Hundreds of Jewish children, from as young as four to eight years old, went across en masse to the 'Aryan side', sometimes several times a day, smuggling food and goods back into the ghettos; the goods often weighed more than the child carrying the load. Smuggling was often the only source of subsistence for the ghetto's inhabitants and without this trade, the inhabitants would have died of starvation.

They were living their lives in a ghetto cut off from the rest of the city, surrounded by three metre high walls topped with barbed wire, in order to confine the population. The wall had been constructed by prisoners captured solely for the purpose of building the walls.

"What's happening out there today?" Czesław asked himself.

Buildings were on fire within the ghetto. A woman appeared holding a child tightly to her chest, she stood for a minute on the fourth floor balcony. Czesław felt as if he had eye contact with her, could she see him? Czesław shook his head in a gesture to say no to the young girl. Whether she could see Czesław or not, she leapt to her death with the baby wrapped in her arms, she had no choice but to escape the burning tenements.

"The people in the ghetto have weapons? I can hear gunfire. They are firing back at the German soldiers" gasped Czesław.

Shots were fired up to the balcony where Czesław was stood. He was unable able to react, rooted to the spot, not able to believe what he saw. His mind could not cope with these events, which were out of context of his everyday life. What used to be normal in Warsaw was now mixed with horrific events, none of it seemed real anymore. Czesław stood still as lumps of broken brick showered down from above him.

"The Germans do not like witnesses watching them. Come inside before you get shot Czesław!" shouted Władysław.

The German authorities granted 35,000 Jews permission to live in the ghetto. There were at least another 350,000 Jews in hiding on top of the agreed number, with an average of 9.2 persons per room. In October 1942, Heinrich Himmler ordered the destruction of the Warsaw Ghetto and for all of its habitants to be deported to forced labour camps. The German SS and police units tried to carry out deportations from the Ghetto in January 1943. This was unsuccessful, the German escort was attacked, allowing many of the Jews to escape.

As a result, the deportations were temporarily stopped. This gave the residents the confidence and time to prepare for the next deportation attempt. On April 19th 1943, the eve of Passover, the SS units and police forced their way into the Ghetto. The streets of the Ghetto were empty. Most of the residents had gone into the underground hiding places and bunkers that they had constructed in preparation for the Warsaw Ghetto uprising. The Germans were forced to retreat by the Jewish resistance fighters who used pistols and grenades, many of which were homemade. The brave attempts of protecting themselves in the Ghetto held out until the 16th May 1943. This was the largest single revolt by the Jewish people during World War II.

Today was the day that Czesław witnessed the uprising. The soldiers, who had superior numbers and fire power, gained ground slowly, burning the buildings as they pushed forward. There was nowhere to hide for the inhabitants. They were gradually overpowered and forced to leave the Ghetto.

No one would believe that the residents of the ghetto did not want to leave it behind, but it had become comparative safety, the alternative being the forced labour and death camps. The people from the Ghetto were marched down the streets with suitcases and prams full of their belongings. They headed for Pruszków, where cattle rail carriages were parked waiting for them.

The Jews threw their gold rings and necklaces into the gutter, rather than have their possessions taken by the German soldiers.

Some onlookers stood watching, others desperately pushed through the crowds and grabbed the discarded jewellery. They squabbled amongst themselves for the gold laying in the streets gutters.

One poor soul turned to the people watching and warned, "What you see happening to us today will happen to you tomorrow and then who will be there to take your gold?"

Chapter 11

12 months later

Czesław's family received a visit from Władysław. They had not seen him for a long time.
Czesław went to Władysław and they hugged.
"It's been a long time brother" said Czesław.
"I had to stay away to protect you all, to keep the family safe." Władysław explained.
His brother would appear and disappear from the family as he carried out missions to smuggle Jews and repatriate allied airmen over the border. The resistance continued the fight from within Poland. The less their friends and family knew of the soldiers work, the better for their own safety.
"Czesiek," said his brother "I was speaking to Mother and your father. We need your help transporting weapons and food for us."
"But the Russians are almost here, I could see them at the other side of the Wisła river." replied Czesław, hardly being able to believe why his brother's army would jeopardise the prospect of freedom.

"Things have changed Czesiek, the Russians and our government in exile are failing to agree on the Russian role once the Red Army enters Warsaw. We don't know if the Russians will be our allies or take rule as our enemies. There has been talk that

they will become allies with others and start the partitions once more" continued Władysław.
"No, they will be our friends" responded Czesław. His eyes wide, he could not believe what was being said. Czesław just wanted the Germans to go away and for their lives to return to normal. He had been living this terrible life of fear for five long years since he was 13 years old.

"What you see is not always the truth Czesiek. The Russians fail to tell us what happened in the Katyn massacre, where many Polish officers were taken to the woods and shot by the Russian army. If they deny the truth, how can we trust them? What else are they hiding? We need to stabilise control by removing the German army ourselves, before the Russians enter our City. The Russians are still sore about what happened to what they see as their land after the last war, the war your father bravely fought in."
Piotr nodded, the memories flowing back as if it were yesterday. He rubbed the stub of his finger remembering the blast from the grenade that severed it and killed his friend, the friend that he had held in his arms until his bright blue piercing eyes had closed forever.
"We need to fight for Poland. We need to stop the Russians taking everything away from us." said Władysław, who was now looking out of the window to hide the tears in his eyes. The tears embarrassed him; he thought he had no more tears left, he had cried so many times over the carnage he had witnessed.

Piotr recognised Władysław's pain and began to speak for him.
"There has been unease and disputes on the Russian, Polish borders, since the collapse of the Austro-Hungarian Empire following the end of my battles in the last World War. We have had a difficult but civil relationship with Russia since the last war, but since the recent annexation by Russia in the Eastern areas of Poland, the militant Ukrainian nationalist extremists have taken advantage of the situation and begun a genocide battle to remove the Polish people from what they believe is their land. Killing young children, much younger than you Czesiek, they have raped and killed innocent civilians. If that was your mother injured or killed how would you feel Czesiek? These actions cannot be left unanswered."

"Listen to your father, Czesiek, he is a wise learned man, he knows what is happening in the world" said his brother.
"I know I believe you both, but I'm not trained in fighting" said Czesław. He still could not believe that the Russians would hurt them. Everyone had been so happy listening to the stories of the advance of the Russian army. Just last night he could hear the close proximity of explosions and gunshots against the occupying German forces. He had seen German soldiers starting to leave Warsaw, surely it was nearly over.

The Russians had got so close, they could be seen on the other side of the Vistula (Wisła) River.

When Stalin received information about the uprising in Warsaw, (Powstanie Warszawskie,) started by the Home Army, the (Armia Krajowa,) he ordered his troops to stop their advance immediately and to withdraw. Was Joseph Stalin's plan to let the resistance liberation operation fail and allow the Armia Krajowa to be crushed? Was this due to his general mistrust of people's actions? Joseph Stalin's name meant *man of steel*, he chose this name himself; he was born Loseb Besarionis dze jughashvili. It was suggested that Stalin suffered from paranoia. He thought his colleagues were plotting to destroy him and as a result of his state of mind, he had many of his senior officers executed. Having executed these officers, there was a lack of experienced senior members with battle knowledge. Stalin made many of the battle plans without guidance, which led to many battle defeats during the Second World War and enormous casualties in Stalin's Red Army. Winston Churchill pleaded with Stalin and America's Roosevelt to help the resistance operation in Warsaw, with no effect and consequently took the matter into his own hands. Without Soviet air clearance, he sent over 200 low level supply drops using the Royal Air Force, the South African Air Force and Polish Air Force, in an operation known as The Warsaw Airlift. The Airlift had to travel a great distance to get to Warsaw, without support from the Red Army, despite the soviet air base being only a five minutes' flight away. The Airlift helped the resistance, who gained ground and managed to cross the Vistula pushing the German army back. However, with lack of support from Stalin's Red Army, the German army began to regain confidence and regrouped to take on the Home Army. The Uprising was the largest battle taken on by any resistance army in the Second World War. The events began on Tuesday 1st August 1944 and the battle raged for 63 days until Monday 2nd October 1944.

It is estimated that 16,000 members of the Polish resistance were killed, in addition to 150,000 Polish civilians who died mostly by way of execution. Jewish people that had been harboured by the Polish inhabitants were discovered by the SS German soldiers who were given the task of the house-to house clearances. A murderous SS brigade, led by Oskar Dirlewanger, was sent to give support to the house clearances of Warsaw. He arrived with only 865 enlisted men and was given a further 1,900 of the most dangerous convicts made up of rapists, paedophiles and murderers who were used to terrorise the population. The criminals greatly boosted Dirlewanger's military numbers and in return for their participation, they were granted release from their life imprisonment sentence. Among the criminals were some poachers; Dirlewanger liked poachers, as they were good at setting traps and were experienced in using rifles. He had previously led his highly notorious heinous SS unit in many campaigns of terror, especially in Belarus. Acting on orders directly from Reichsführer SS

Heinrich Himmler, Dirlewanger's soldiers were given free rein to pillage and murder the civilians of Warsaw. The whole city of Warsaw was to be levelled to the ground and the SS brigade began with their house by house clearances.
Dirlewanger's Brigade were intent on killing anyone they found and were credited with killing 30,000 civilians in two days in the Wola district of Warsaw. In one instance, when the Brigade went to a children's orphanage, 300 infants were beaten to death with rifle butts; Dirlewanger had given a direct order to the SS soldiers not to waste bullets on the defenseless children.

Czesław, along with his lifelong friends, Waldek, Jurek, Bernek and Janek, had been in the battle dodging bullets and negotiating bomb craters all day in their role of helping to put out fires, transporting injured soldiers and moving ammunition to where it was needed. The light was diminishing as the evening arrived. They were carrying wounded soldiers back to an old warehouse where there was one doctor and 15 volunteer nurses from the Red Cross. They were trying to help the wounded and dying at a temporary frontline hospital.
There was no normality in Czesław's life now, he no longer had a job to go to, the city was locked down in battle.
Nine weeks ago, he had set-off with his father and Waldek on their usual route to work, when they heard the sound of gunshots. The three stopped in their tracks.

"Wait here" said Piotr "Press yourself against the wall and stay crouched down low. Wait for me here."

Piotr, slowly and cautiously, walked to the end of the block of buildings. He looked around the corner and saw others in the same situation, stood with their backs against the walls of the properties, all smartly dressed in suits and long coats. A young girl in school uniform held her mother's hand, they were both crouched down and the girl was crying hysterically. The mother looked at Piotr, fear in her eyes, not knowing what to do.

"Go back the way you came" said Piotr, "You must go home."

The two remained where they were, unable to move. Piotr crawled over to the mother and child, they were frozen to the spot with fear.

"Come with me." Piotr picked up the little girl and gently held her. She stopped crying and looked into Piotr's eyes. "No school today for you, little one." Piotr led them both away from the noise. "Now go home. From today there are no more routines, we will have to adapt and survive."

The mother led her child back to relative safety, she tuned to Piotr and said "Dziękuję za życzliwość."

They put down the stretcher between them, both exhausted, hungry and thirsty. Faces and hands blackened by the debris of the battlefield. Czesław gazed at Waldek, rivulets of sweat had run down his face leaving sooty streaks where the sweat had washed away the brick dust and grime.

Their hands were red with other people's blood.

"No more!" ordered the nurse, "We have no more room."

"We can't leave him on the street" reasoned Czesław, looking down at the soldier they had carried through the mayhem. The soldier's arm had flesh blown away exposing bone and blood vessels. A leather belt from the soldier's own trousers had been wrapped around what was left of his arm to stem the flow of precious blood pumping from his broken body. A bullet had struck his elbow when he had been holding his weapon ready to take a shot. The bullet had entered at the elbow and tracked along the bone and entered his chest cavity at the armpit. The blood had soaked his jacket, blood was frothing from his mouth and he was struggling to breathe with only one functioning lung. His chest moved rapidly, shallow breaths, his brain was dosing his body with endorphins and adrenaline, the body's natural mechanism to cope with damage. He was going into shock, his brain was crying out for oxygen forcing his one working lung to ventilate his damaged body and supply the oxygen required. His heart was pumping like a train to assist the flow of oxygenated blood. The soldier smiled at the boys and tried to speak. It was difficult to understand at first. Czesław placed his ear as close as possible to the soldier's mouth and felt warm damp spray on his cheek as the soldier tried to speak again. "Danke, ich schulde dir mein Leben." Czesław could not speak German, but knew what he was saying. He and his friends were not without feeling, they were helping all the wounded.

Czesław's eyes burnt as tears tried to wash away the brick dust from his bloodshot, tear-filled eyes. Czesław turned to face the soldier and replied "Nie ma za co."
The two boys tried to keep low as they ran back to the not so obvious frontline. Positions constantly changed with gains and losses of ground.
Czesław carried the wounded German soldier's weapon under his arm.
They picked up some rounds, which were good for the rifle, from a dead German soldier that lay at an awkward unnatural angle in the debris of what used to be a stone wall. The very wall Waldek used to sit on waiting for Czesław to join him when they used to play out together. That all seemed a lifetime away now.
Czesław remembered the trips with his friends to Wilanów, a beautiful district of Warsaw with a magnificent palace, the Polish Versailles. It had gold and cream walls with a green roof. The tram trips were fun, singing and playing their instruments. Czesław remembered the large grassed area, the smell of freshly mown grass where they would sit as a group under the shade of a large leafy tree...
A gunshot sounded. The dead body of the soldier shuddered, the bullet reemerged and hit the tumbled down wall, shattering the stone work, Czesław was dashed with shattered stone dust, it felt like a sandstorm, he tasted the powdered stone in his mouth, his eyes and ears were filled with the debris.
"Better move quick" advised Czesław.

A sniper had spotted them collecting the badly needed ammunition.
"That sniper wants us dead" said Waldek.
A Polish soldier spotted them, he ran over to where they were.
"We are going to be overrun at this position" said the soldier. They recognised the resistance fighter armband, he shouted to be heard above the noise of war. "Don't come back to this position. We are moving to Starówka, we will fight to our death there."
The Old Town, Starówka, was established in the 13th century. Initially surrounded by an earthwork rampart, now it had tall stone walls. This was a tactical move by the Resistance. There they could engage the larger number of German troops in the narrow streets of a closely built-up area. It would make the task for German troops more difficult to flush out the resistance fighters there. The large tanks would find it difficult to manoeuvre in the confines of the beautiful Old Town.
"Take this" said Czesław. He handed over the ammunition and rifle that they had recovered to the soldier.
"Niemiecki! Nie ma prolemu, to jest dobre. Do widzenia pryzyjacielu"
No sooner had the words registered in their ears, the soldier had gone, silent and quick.
Back at the emergency medical centre, things were not improving.
"Make yourselves useful. Move the dead outside to make room for us to work on the living" instructed the nurse. Her face had smears of blood

from where she had, without a second thought, touched her face when moving her long blond hair back from her face, her blue eyes were fierce. She was not much older than Czesław but she was mature beyond her years. Her pretty face broke into a smile, she was sorry for being so abrupt with the two boys, but she was losing her own battle amongst the casualties here.
Czesław did not know who to choose in his task. "What if they were still alive?" thought Czesław. The young nurse had read his thoughts, "BOYS! Here and here"
The bodies had been bandaged, covering their wounds. Great care had been made to make them comfortable in their last moments of life, many could not be saved from their catastrophic injuries. Limbs missing from the impact of mortar shells, high velocity boat tailed sniper rounds that crushed bone and severed limbs.
"The indignity of death" thought Czesław looking around him; mouths open, eyes staring, heads raked back at an irregular angle. Rigors had started to take hold.
Rigor mortis 'stiffness of death' starts at the head, opening the eyelids first and stiffening the neck, all within the first couple of hours of death. The stiffening continues down the body, to the arms and finally the legs after several hours.
Some of the bodies were curled in a ball, they had been nursing stomach injuries. Czesław and Waldek picked up the corpses in this foetal position, they could not possibly be straightened.
A soldier with a resistance armband entered the

building, sweating from exertion, chest heaving. He had to compose himself for a couple of seconds to get air into his lungs to make his announcement. He was covered in brick dust, his face blackened with dirt from the fight. His eyes wild, wide with fear. Yes, fear, everyone feels fear. Controlling the feeling of fear is the mark of a brave individual. He had made his visit to help the medical staff. He was not going to flee, he would return to his brothers in arms until his death.

"Leave! You must all leave this place, we are overrun. Go home to your families you need to go now" he commanded.

The doctor, who was a Polish army officer, agreed with him. He spoke out to his exhausted faithful helpers, the Red Cross nurses. "You must all leave. I will stay and look after the wounded here. Soldier, thank you for your bravery, you must leave us now, for if the enemy find you here with us, they will kill us all."

The medical staff knew they were in great danger, but their training and ethics gave them the strong resolve to stay with the casualties.

Czesław and his friends could do no more, their job was done here. They ran back to the tenements, like homing pigeons they almost flew. They did not feel the uneven broken rubble beneath their feet. They ran and ran, keeping close together, keeping low. This way of travelling had become normality, low and fast.

The doctor could see soldiers approaching the warehouse. He asked one of the nurses to cut down a white bed sheet to make into a surrender flag.

"We must surrender this place now. There are German soldiers outside the building. They will not hurt you, you are not soldiers, you are no threat to them as civilians. Stay calm, no sudden movements."

The SS soldiers were Dirlewanger's soldiers. The doctor and the nurse with the improvised white flag opened the doors to show their surrender flag. The SS soldiers ran into the building with bayonets fixed. The doctor and nurses pleaded with the soldiers not to harm the wounded. They were surrendering to the soldiers.

The injured German soldiers repeated the doctor and nurses pleas in German.

One account about that evening was told by Mathias Schenk, an 18-year-old who served as a Strumpionier, an assault engineer. He was assigned to Dirlewanger's brigade because of his knowledge of explosives. His task was to open and allow access to properties for Dirlewanger's heinous brigade to enter the buildings.

This young man described what he saw.

"The soldiers came across a makeshift hospital. The doors opened for us and a nurse appeared with a tiny white flag. We went inside the building with bayonets fixed. There were Polish and German wounded soldiers lying side by side. The Polish officer, a doctor and 15 Polish Red Cross nurses surrendered the military hospital to us. They begged the soldiers not to kill the wounded, but they would not listen, they were breaking heads with rifle butts. When their killing frenzy ended the Dirlewanger's ran after the nurses, they were ripping clothes off them. We were sent outside to stand on guard duty, we could hear women screaming. In the evening the nurses were sent through the square with their hands on their heads. Blood ran down their legs. The doctor was dragged along behind with a noose around his neck, he had a crown of thorns on his head. The nurses were led to the gallows. Dirlewanger approached one of the nurses who already had a noose around her neck and was stood on a pile of bricks. Dirlewanger kicked away the bricks that she was standing on, he just laughed."

The five boys stopped and stood outside the tenements, feeling some false sense of security in that they were home. The noise of war was still with them, screams, mortar rounds, explosions, the cracking and smashing of anything in the path of the missiles. Being home made the disaster feel a little more distant. They shook hands in such a formal way and said their goodbyes

"Mieć dobre życie" said Czesław to his lifelong friends.

This had become the way in the past few days. There were no more 'see you laters', later may never happen. The bonds of friendship had become very intense in their times of hardship.

The boys did sense the impending doom, this was the early hours of Thursday the 14th September 1944.

Chapter 12

Czesław entered the cellar room below the tenements. They had all been living in the cellar area since the start of the uprising. His mother and father were sat in the dark room waiting for his return. Helena had been asleep on the bed, her head on Piotr's shoulder. She woke startled, arms outstretched before she had woken enough to stand.
She slowly stood up, then unsteadily walked towards Czesław.
"Your face is so dirty, your clothes are filthy, you must get cleaned up." She hugged her son, the dirt transferring to her own clean clothes, silent tears from Czesław, shoulders heaving and sobbing from Helena. Piotr watched the strong bond between mother and son, it reminded him of when he had returned from the war, his own mother had greeted him sobbing. "Don't worry Mother, I'm alive," Piotr had uttered to his mother "but so many of my friends have gone."

Loud speakers sparked up outside of the tenements. Czesław was eating after his quick wash with a face cloth and water out of a container. His father was washing up in a bowl, his mother drying and putting things tidily to one side. Everything was rushed, the feeling of being safe had gone. Their lives were about to change forever.

"All residents hear this...all residents hear this..." Piotr went to the doorway. Mrs. Tortoise was there also, they briefly acknowledged each other with a nod. They both focussed their attention on the uniformed men in the half light of the early dawn. "You have twenty minutes to collect your belongings, you need to take clothing to travel. After twenty minutes soldiers will enter these buildings to set the buildings on fire. You must be out of the buildings in twenty minutes or you will burn with the building." The announcement was made in perfect Polish.

The population in the annexed Polish territories had been conscripted forcibly into the Wehrmacht army in Upper Silesia and in Pomerania. They were declared citizens of the Third Reich by law and were subject to a drumhead court-martial in the case of refusing to join the German army. Any refusal would be treated as a draft evasion, punishable by being taken to a death camp along with their families. Some of conscripts, a minority, considered themselves as German due to living in areas previously under German rule prior to the First World War. They would join the German army without any feeling of betrayal to Poland. The soldiers stood waiting near their vehicles, making ready the Einstossflammenwerfer 46. The flamethrower was a mechanical incendiary device designed to project a long, controllable stream of flaming fuel. The clang of metal could be heard as cans of fuel were being unloaded from the wagons. The normally peaceful cul-de-sac was full of noise

and echoing voices.
Piotr remembered these terrible weapons, he had encountered them in his battles. He always thought we have the Greeks to thank for this weapon, he had remembered from his history lessons at school. Flamethrowers were first used by the Greeks in the 1st Century AD.
They left the cellar and quickly made their way up to their apartment to gather what they could.
Piotr could hear Czesław calling him,
"What about your lovely records Father?"
Czesław could not bear to leave all his father's records behind.
 "Rause, Rause!" soldiers shouted from across the square. Soldiers were now running up the concrete stairways, their boots drumming on the concrete steps that led to the upper floors, lugging the heavy cylinders on their backs, hoses in hand ready to commence the deed. They had already started to set alight the tenements opposite Czesław's block of flats. The residents could be seen fleeing, possessions in their hands, racing along the walkways. The noise of the flame guns propelling the ignited fluid could be heard as a roar, like the stories of the Vistula river Wawel dragon breathing flames. Cries and sobbing could be heard from the flats opposite. The soldiers were starting at the top most floors and working systematically down, so as not to cut off their own exit from the burning building.
"We must leave now Helena, Czesiek, no more time left. Come on son."
 Czesław was still in his bedroom checking in case

he had left something he would regret leaving. He saw his much loved skates in the cupboard, he loved his skates and all the good times he had with his friends skating at the park.
He quickly grabbed his mouth harmonica and placed it safely in his jacket inside pocket.
He appeared in the hallway with one of his mother and father's favourite records and silver tray.
"Thank you Czesiek, but we can't carry that as well. All you need is warm clothing and your suit, you will need those." said Helena.
She gently took the tray from Czesław and placed it on the floor. A wedding present from Piotr's mother. Helena put her hand out for Czesław to pass her the record, her eyes welled up as she held it to her chest. Paweł Prokopieni - Wieriowoczka, 1933, a Russian song, sung by a Polish singer, Helena could imagine herself dancing with Piotr at the Warsaw ballroom, Piotr in his black suit, white shirt and bow tie, her in a Molyneux couture pale blue crepe evening gown. It all could have been yesterday.
"Come along, we must leave now Czesiek" Helena turned to go hiding her tearful face.
"Take the photographs, we cannot leave these behind" pleaded Czesław.
Czesław stood on the communal landing looking at the apartment, the door was open,
Should he close it and lock it? Piotr stepped forward. He looked over his shoulder and saw the tenements opposite already burning,
"Let's make it a bit more difficult for them." He pulled the door to the frame, the lock clunked

closed. Piotr winked at Czesław.
Czesław looked up at the closed door and read out loud "Number 19."
Piotr turned to his family and said "We have each other, we do not need anything else. We must go now."
They walked along the communal walkway together. Czesław in the middle like when he was a young child walking with his parents. Czesław looked back at the apartment door for the last time, he felt so anxious.
"Come now Czesiek there is nothing we can do here" said Piotr.
Czesław had a picture of himself in a soldier's uniform with his father and his uncle, he made them stop so he could put it in his mother's suitcase. They were outside Mrs.Tortoises's flat, the door was open, he could not help but look in, he could hear sobbing, "She is still in there" said Czesław.
Piotr went in to the flat. "Come with us. We must leave our homes now."
They all left together. Czesław could see the tenements opposite burning, black smoke billowed from the broken glass panes which cracked and broke in the intense heat, people's personal possessions added fuel to the flames, years of possessions burning. Memories, photographs, burning. This could not be happening, was this real or a nightmare?
Czesław got to the stairway. German voices sounded in the basement, "Rause, Rause" His heartbeat quickened, his breathing noisy, he could

hear his own heartbeat pounding in his head.
Czesław joined his mother and father and other neighbours in the entrance. They were huddled together in a group as if waiting for a final family photo.
"Rause, Rause, the young people will be going to Germany for work, the older people will remain in Poland."
"Czesiek take this." Helena opened her full to bursting case and pulled out a warm coat belonging to Piotr. "Put this in your case, it can get very cold in Germany in winter."
Czesław took the coat, his father was nodding in agreement.
They left the block together, Helena was slightly ahead as they left the courtyard following the group along the narrow road that led to the main road. They passed the soldiers and their wagons; troop carriers and wagons with petrol cylinders. Soldiers pointed them towards the main road.
"You! …You two come here."
A soldier pointed at Czesław and Piotr
"Yes, you two come here!"
They both walked obediently, yet cautiously towards a portly unshaven old boy in his fifties. His right hand thumb as thick as a Vieska salami, was visible tucked behind the leather strap that held a rifle with a large bolt on it. Czesław had picked up a similar rifle from an injured German soldier that very morning. Czesław could smell alcohol on the soldier's rancid breath, along with a mix of nicotine.
The soldier motioned to them to follow, without

even checking to see if they were still there. They crossed the main road behind the soldier and followed him along the track that led to stables. Piotr and Czesław looked at each other and then back at the main group. The main group were following each other in a line, following the contour of the wall adjacent the footpath on the main road. Czesław felt very alone leaving the crowd, they were both isolated from the main group.
"Come" ordered the soldier.
Czesław remembered the chickens that used to be feeding in the grass and dirt of the path, some turning and walking away with nervous clucks as Czesław approached running along the track, eagerly wanting to reach the stable where the large brown horse was kept. Today there was no sign of any other life on the track, the track that dipped then rises with a mound to the right. There was no sign of the majestic horse in the stable which used to greet Czesław. It had long since been taken away to join the war effort to pull along the artillery guns which were mounted on large carts and dragged to the warfront. The stable door was open, swung right back on its hinges, the top split section of the stable door had come off its hinges and was laid on the floor in the dirt where it had fallen. Czesław looked at the dark opening, wondering if the stable boy's large barrow was still in there. No sounds from inside, no red faced stable boy. They were all alone. The soldier's dusty black boots kicked up the pebbles as he lumbered on in front of them. The soldier stopped

and motioned them to walk past him.
"YOU!" he shouted, pointing at Piotr.
"Stand there on the raised mound. You boy, carry straight onto the stable wall."
 As Czesław approached the open barn doorway he could smell the familiar scent of straw from the stable door opening. The strong ammonia smell of horse urine was not as strong as he had remembered, but it was still there. Scents and smells are strong memory triggers. They can take you back in an instant to a moment in time, even to memories from many years ago, the memory of it will be as vivid as it ever was.
Piotr stood on the raised mound, he was beginning to worry, this was not right, he thought they had been summoned to collect or clean something, but now he was worried for their safety.
"You boy, stop! Turn around and face me. You over there, look at your son."
The soldier grunted with the effort as he removed the rifle from his shoulder. His uniform was dirty and torn, cigarette stub in his mouth, a cloud of smoke hid his face as he exhaled. He stubbed out the cigarette on the wood side of the rifle just above the trigger guard. He placed the stub behind his right ear for later, then lifted and placed the wooden stock against his right shoulder and pushed the end of the stock firmly against the woolen jacket, he adjusted his feet to create a steady platform for the rifle.
Piotr struggled to swallow, his mouth was dry, his heartbeat was raised, he could hear the thud, thud, of his fast pumping heart in his ears, his adrenalin

had kicked in. The fight or flight response was being activated in his body, yet he just stood and watched in horror, looking at the scruffy soldier then his defenseless son who looked so alone, stood there with his back to the barn wall. He could see the colour had drained from Czesław's face, he stood still, no sound, he wondered if his son knew what was going to happen. Piotr knew the damage the Mauser would cause when it delivered the deadly metal round into his son's body. His own battle friends had died blood pumping from a bullets entry and exit wounds. Piotr mouthed his name "Czesiek", from his dry lips, no sound was emitted. His son looked so defenseless, so vulnerable, like the day he was born. Piotr had cradled him then, in his arms as a newborn baby, tightly wrapped in a towel. He had vowed that he would not allow anyone to harm his son. But today he stood still, he did not protest to the soldier, he did nothing, "What kind of father am I?" he thought.

Czesław focussed his eyes on the barrel of the rifle, the sight was moving wildly, then began to steady. The background behind the soldier became blurred, sound from the crowds muted, all that could be heard was the soldier grunting like a wheezing bulldog, breathing through its restricted airways. The soldier focussed on the foresight, then made sure the rear sight was level with the front sight, his feet adjusted again as though he had all the time in the world. This soldier was enjoying this, savouring the moment.

Czesław focused on the barrel, then on the

soldier's chunky right-hand forefinger on the trigger.

As his finger took up first pressure on the trigger, the finger whitened, Czesław closed his eyes, his stomach felt like it was ascending up to his throat, his throat tightened, he could no longer swallow. Czesław waited for the bullet to pierce his skin and break his body, no sounds now other than his own heartbeat loud in his head. Would it be a bullet in the head? It would be over quickly in the head. Or would it be a body shot? That would be a slower and a more painful death. Czesław had seen the damage caused by a round. Sometimes the bullet tracks along the bones and comes out a distance away from the entry hole, smashing bone and severing arteries. What would it be like being dead? Would he see his parents again in the afterlife? He had not been given the chance to say goodbye to them. Would Skrawek be waiting for him? Should he pray?

Suddenly there was a clatter, as the soldiers rifle bounced on the dirt track, the small stones scratching the wood surface and coating it with dust, then a thud almost at the same time and a grunt as the soldier expelled air as his large rotund body hit the ground, hard.

Czesław opened one eye, but the other remained tightly shut, his mouth tightly closed, every muscle in his body contracted in anticipation of the bullets penetration. Another soldier stood above the man in the dirt. The man swore in German at the soldier on the ground, then he spoke perfect Polish, clear and loud.

"You will not kill any of these people. That is not your decision to make."
He held his pistol in his right hand pointing the barrel at the head of the soldier on the floor. There was no tremble in his hand, his hand was steady. The soldier on the floor cursed and swore in German like an old drunken vagrant at the man standing over him.
The man was an SS soldier. His uniform was immaculate, clean, pressed, his SS epaulette visible on his right collar. The SS soldier looked at Czesław and asked "Are you afraid? No, do not be afraid, not of him. Look at him on the ground. He cannot cause any harm to you now."
He then turned to Piotr. "Go now with your son, I will deal with this soldier."
Czesław looked at his father, his father's face as pale as death itself. Piotr was in shock, he could not move. Czesław ran to his father and physically pushed him to make his father's body kick back in to action,
"Go now, take your jackets off so that no one can recognise you again. Split up, join the crowd, I can't be with you to protect you...go now."
They both hurried back towards the crowd, Czesław at the rear still pushing Piotr along. Czesław felt a flow of emotion, he wanted to laugh and cry at the same time. Czesław thought how they had not even thanked the SS man that had saved their lives. Half turning to look where they had run from, Czesław uttered the words "Dziękuję."

Czesław heard gunshots on the street. Two men,

possibly resistance fighters were on the floor laid at an awkward angle against the wall, they had not had the protection of Czesław and Piotr's angel. Czesław could not make any sense of what had just happened to them on the dirt track, he would remember this incident and his SS Guardian Angel for the rest of his life.

The German soldiers on the street were frisking all the younger men and feeling their shoulders for any swelling. Swelling was a crude indicator that the person may have recently fired a rifle. The impact from the rifle butt, when the bullet fires, causes a kick back to the shoulder, causing soft tissue damage with the consequence of a swelling.

"Come Czesiek" Piotr spoke for the first time since the incredulous chain of events. They both joined the main group. It always feels safer to be part of the herd. Piotr was looking ahead trying to find Helena. It was difficult to make her out in the crowd. Had she worn a head scarf?

"Piotr, Czesiek!" Helena had held back when she lost sight of them both. Piotr ran forward and got to her first, Czesław was not in sight.

"Where have you both been? I lost you as we joined the main street, why are they separating people and what are they doing to us?" Helena was in a state of panic. "I was so scared when I lost you both."

"Don't worry Helena, we are together now. Czesiek is close behind me."

Czesław was pushing his way through the crowd, he could see Piotr and Helena together ahead of him.

"Czesiek will not be staying with us Helena, the young ones are going on to work in Germany, all the younger ones are going away"

"Mother, Father I'm here. I can't stay long I have to go." said Czesław, panting, more from shock than exertion. "Here is your case Czesiek, I kept them all together when you both disappeared."

Helena opened one of the suitcases.

"Take some more warm clothes from my case, it will be cold where you are going" said Helena, fussing over him, her little, big boy.

"Here take my engagement ring, you can use it to buy food." Helena raised her arm to reduce the blood flow to her hand so she could ease the ring off over her finger, her fingers had widened over the years since their engagement, making it more difficult to remove the precious ring from her finger.

Piotr raised his coat sleeve to remove his watch.

"Here, take my watch, you don't want to be late on your first day in your new work." Piotr fumbled to remove his watch from under his coat sleeve. Piotr had received it from his own father for his 21st birthday.

"I can't take your memories" protested Czesław.

He knew how precious these items were to his parents. People did not have a great number of possessions, but what they had meant so much to them.

"Thank you so much, I love you both." Czesław

kissed them one by one.

"I will contact you both when I get to Germany I promise." Czesław held his mother close like he never wanted to let her go.

"Tata, goodbye for now, kocham was oboje."

"We love you too Son" Piotr replied, looking into his sons eyes. He had nearly lost him to the trigger happy soldier and now he was losing his son again.

"Take this handkerchief Czesiek, so I can see you waving." said Helena.

Czesław picked up his heavy case with both hands on the handle, he turned to follow the long line of young men and women setting off on their new venture to work in Germany. He turned and could see his mother waving, white handkerchief in hand. Czesław stopped and waived back with his handkerchief. He hoped he would see his mother and father again soon, when all this mess was sorted out. They would never be able to return to the tenements, they were destroyed. He could see the smoke rising from their home from where he stood. All of Warsaw appeared to be on fire. Gunshots sounded from the location of the Old Town in the distance. Maybe his brother was there? Czesław could picture him, calm, responding to events as they happened, proud to be doing what he knew was right. Czesław briefly stopped, there was a man laid on the floor. Czesław had rescued men like this, just a few hours ago. Blood oozing from their punctured jackets. A German soldier saw Czesław looking at the blooded corpse.

"Take his boots. Look they are wasted on a dead man."

Czesław broke away from the soldier's gaze. He could not help thinking that this could have been how he himself would have looked after being shot by the drunken soldier at the stable yard. How is it that I am still alive? Who was the guardian angel? Where had he come from? None of it made any sense to him.

The crowd of people were being directed down the same route that the Jews had followed the previous year, when the ghettos were being cleared. They were heading to Pruszków. A voice close to his ear distracted him from his thoughts,

"Where are you going? Jump over the wall. Come over here" said an older man.

"No it's fine, I'm off to work in Germany" replied Czesław, following the crowd. They were funnelled towards the railway track. It looked strange, no platform to board from. This was a railway engine repair yard, not a station. Czesław could see the smoke and hissing steam from the engine at the front of cattle trucks. The mass exodus got closer to the track. Czesław held onto his suitcase tightly, this was all that was left of his lifelong belongings. He had no home, no family, he was surrounded and jostled by a sea of strangers. They were all in the same world of pain and sadness. Czesław felt small, vulnerable, totally alone in the crowd .The queue edged forwards handled roughly by soldiers. Some of the people slipped and fell from the trucks onto the floor, they were ignored as the soldiers pushed forward more people. Those already on the cattle truck held out helping hands to aid the others to climb onboard. Czesław threw his case up to the carriage floor and started to heave his upper body on to the dusty dirty wooden floor.

"There's not enough room" objected Czesław.

The soldiers ignored his protest, they continued pushing more people up behind Czesław. The truck had the aroma of an old barn, very much like the farm sheds he used to go to swap spirits for food in the countryside. Those were exciting but scary days. Czesław looked around, everyone had suitcases, some people were crying, some shouting, it was hot and difficult to breathe in the humidity of the carriage, he placed his case between his legs.

Finally the shuffling of feet stopped and the doorway opening darkened as the doors closed. Before the light was completely blocked out, Czesław looked at his father's watch, partly for comfort, he was glad to have something from his family with him, it was 12 noon. He was already tired, he had not been to bed, he had been pushed out of his home at first light. The horror of the stable courtyard played through his mind.

Czesław took a deep breath, inhaling the humid stagnant air, he forced his mind to think of something else. He looked around the darkened cattle wagon as his eyes became accustomed to the dark. There was a jolt as the engine took the strain of the weight, the carriage wheels squeaked in protest as the train started to slowly move forwards. Czesław could not see outside, there were no windows.

After a couple of hours the train felt like it was slowing. The crowd were pushed off balance, they could not fall, due to the number of bodies packed onboard. The train slowed more and then stopped. One of the passengers frantically started to pull up a loose board on the truck floor, then another and squeezed himself through the tiny gap.

"No," warned another passenger "you will get hurt or get us in to trouble."

The man had made his mind up, he ignored the pleas of his fellow passengers as he lay down on the sleepers and ballast on the track below the carriage. Czesław looked on thinking the man must be mad. He was going to Germany to work, it was not worth dying for, trying to escape. The train jolted and started to move on again. The man that had pleaded with the escapee replaced the boards to cover the escape hole. The escape artist's suitcase remained on the train, everyone's eyes were on the case, all alone, abandoned.

After another ten minutes the train stopped again. Everyone stood quiet not knowing what was happening. One of the passengers cracked open the sliding door, daylight and fresh air poured into the crowded truck. "Where are we?" asked the passenger to a man below them dressed in a dark blue boiler suit and canvas dark blue jacket. He had a long handled mallet in his hands, black oily smudges on his face. "Don't you know where you are?" he replied, incredulous of the question. "You are all entering the death camp."

There was an audible gasp in unison from the passengers that had heard the words of the track man. Everyone at the same time repeated the last two words spoken by the track man, "Death camp."

"No!" Czesław cried out loud, "I am going for work in Germany, there is some mistake. He does not know what he is talking about."

Chapter 13

Czesław

The train started to move forward again. Everyone stood in stunned silence. We were no longer passengers bound for Germany, we were prisoners in our own country.

We passed under a sign bearing the words 'Arbeit Mach Frei' the German ethic meaning 'work sets you free'.

The truck doors were opened from the outside, the passengers were ordered to leave the trucks. People automatically obeyed without question. They slipped, jumped, fell onto the cobbled area. We could see the walls and the towers ahead of us.

"This is a mistake, I must be on the wrong train."

Czesław was going through an escalated shock scenario. Shock, disbelief, anger, denial.

I moved forward with the rest of the group, carrying our heavy suitcases.

The escapee's suitcase was still in the truck, alone. Everyone had disembarked stepping over or kicking the abandoned suitcase out of the way. I could still picture the escapee man's face as he disappeared through the hole in the floor, beads of sweat, bright red cheeks. He had dark hair receding at the top, thick hair at the sides with a thick moustache. I could imagine him laid on his back looking up at the others in the truck, finger on lips, begging for silence from the onlookers.

The long line made its way towards a building that stood detached from the main buildings. A slightly built man, in a dark green tunic and an SS cap, tilted to one side watching the crowd walking towards him, the SS officer indicated which side I should pass him on using his cane. I passed him to his right.

I noticed the man's polished boots. The officer stood with his thumb tucked into the belt of the pistol holster, a cane in his other hand. He suddenly raised his voice.

Startled, I turned, but he dismissed me by a wave of the gloved hand that had been tucked in his belt.

"You!" commanded the officer "Pass on my left." He flicked his cane indicating which side the family beside me should pass him.

I stood in a queue with a fellow Post Office colleague, whom I recognised. He was quite a bit older than me, about 38, I was 18. I looked up at him and said "This is a mistake, we are going for work in Germany, we will not be here long. They will put us back on the train soon to go to work."

He looked down at me, but did not answer. "I was told by the German soldiers that we were going to Germany for work, just this morning, as they told us to leave our homes. My parents gave me some warm clothes, they said it could be cold in

Germany at this time of year."

I looked up at my colleague waiting for a response.

He walked on as if he had not heard my encouraging view of what was happening.

We entered a building, a Polish speaking official with an armband on took hold of my suitcase.

"No!" I protested "I need this case, I have warm clothes and all my personal belongings in there."

The official was very sympathetic, "Don't worry, your case will be over there." He motioned towards a large pile of suit cases. "It will stay there, you can have it back whenever you leave."

I looked at my colleague's face who was next to me. An expression of 'see I told you so' was written all over his face, with eyebrows raised, no smile.

We both sat down together to give our details, name, address, age, employment, health. A doctor stamped the paper to qualify that I was fit and did not need medical care. Date stamped 14th September 1944 .The official reached out and gently took hold of my wrist.

"Watch." demanded the official.

"It's my father's" I protested.

"Watch please. We will keep your valuables safe here in this building."

I thought about my mother's ring in my breast pocket and my gold chain that was around my neck. Should I hand those in for safe keeping? On second thoughts, maybe not, I did not trust these men. We were then directed to the showers and issued with striped pyjamas and a hat.

We had numbers issued I was prisoner number 197932.

"Remove all your clothes, take a shower and then put on your uniforms."

I placed my mother's ring on the gold chain hung next to the crucifix and placed it around my neck for safe keeping.

I followed the procedure on autopilot, without knowing that this was the first stage of my institutionalisation. Shower, number one haircut, dental check, uniform.

A man with an armband showing some authority approached me as I left the dentist following my checkup. He stood in front blocking my way, his eyes were on what was hung around my neck.

"You have something around your neck" he got closer invading my personal space.

"A ring, gold chain, crucifix…give them to me and I'll give you some bread."

"What! Do you think that I am mad or something? I can't give you these precious items for a piece of bread!"

"Put it this way," said the official in perfect Polish. "You give them to me, I give you some bread. If you go into the barracks with your gold, someone will give you a good beating and take them from you and you will not get any food in return."

I tentatively took the bread, my hand was trembling as I handed over my precious belongings, which had been given to me as a christening gift and my mother's engagement ring.

"They don't believe in God in there. In the barracks they would kill you and take it from your corpse" he warned.

I wished my mother and father were here. They would know best what I should do. I received a fifteen centimetre bread roll, it was thrust forward by the thief. I noticed that the man's finger nails had enough dirt to grow potatoes under them and he was holding my bread.

"Here, hide this under your jacket, you don't want anyone to steal it do you? And put your cap on" advised the thief. "You will be beaten by the guards for not wearing it."

I half thought to thank him for his caring advice, but no, I realised I did not owe this man any thanks. I had paid him too much already.

I watched as the thief placed my family's possessions in a pocket which had a triangle on it.

The thief saw me looking down at the red inverted triangle on his jacket; it looked like an upside down road stop sign on the left breast pocket of his jacket.

"Yes, they all have a meaning, they are badges of shame" he told me.

"You like me are Schutzhäftlinge. A political prisoner, a saboteur, an enemy of the state. The Jewish prisoners wear the Star of David, a pink triangle for Homosexual prisoners, green triangles are criminal prisoners berufsverbrecher, be careful around them, they are hard men. Black triangles with the letter Z for Gypsies, purple triangles Bibelforscher-Vereinigung for Jehovah's Witnesses and Baptists. They are all enemies of the state because of their pacifistic beliefs."

The man laughed, just like the villain in the pantomimes that my father used to take me to around Christmas time.

"Go now!" he barked.

With a flick of his head, he gestured for me to go on my way. My precious items were now gone, spent. I would not get any more information from this individual.

I walked over to a large group of men that sat on the floor waiting to be allocated accommodation huts. As we sat there my Post Office colleague joined us. He walked around and sat behind me, he leant forward to speak in to my ear, "Well...are you still going to Germany for work?"

The reality hit as hard as if I had received a sledge hammer blow to the head.

One by one they stood up as the coolness of the evening approached, they started to walk to keep warm.

I saw my friends in the crowd, I felt no longer

alone, I ran over to them, "Jurek, Janek, Waldemar my friend and Bernek, you are here too."

"You know nothing can keep the Warsaw boys apart" jested Waldek.

We were all told to stand and pay attention for a smartly dressed SS Soldier who stood in front of the crowd on a raised platform; the peak of his hat covering his eyes as he gave an introduction, a not so welcome speech.

"I am Rudolf Höss. You are detained in my camp until further notice."

These words dashed any hopes I had. I felt sick that I had been so taken in. The postal engineer had seen through it from the start. So if he had known, why had he not tried to escape like the man on the cattle wagon that had disappeared through the hole in the floor? I felt that this was the end of my world.

The groups were allocated to the brick three storey buildings. Each line of people filed off to walk into the buildings. Inside, the buildings were fitted out with three-tier bunks. The bunks were in long lines, very close together; they consisted of wooden bases with a straw-filled mattress to lie on. There were two wood stoves with brick chimneys for heat, stood at each end of the long rooms. I climbed up to the top bunk, there was no allocation. I wanted to be at the top, out of the way. Soon I was joined by two other prisoners. No words were said, we were all in shock.

We were all told not to leave our bunks. I laid on the bunk and took the most expensive piece of bread in the world out of my jacket, where I had hidden it. I took one bite out of the bread that I had bought with my family's possessions. I had not eaten since breakfast. Was that today? It seemed like days ago. Just this morning I had been with my loving father and mother. Mother had made sure we were all fed at breakfast. Father had washed up. Washed and tidied up and for what? It had all been set on fire by the soldiers with their petrol flame throwers. My thoughts churned over in my mind. Did I do the right thing giving away the precious jewellery given to me by my parents? If only my parents were with me now. I felt so scared and alone.

Would they be annoyed with me? Well it was done now, I had taken the most expensive bite of bread that I had ever taken in my life. It was dry with a hard crust.

I looked around at the others next to me. Was the bread seller lying, would these people around me steal my precious jewellery? Everyone was in the same predicament, no one would surely steal from each other. Maybe the bread seller was a liar, just like the German soldiers that had assured us all that we were going to work in Germany.

Would there have been riots in the streets if the people had known the truth? They had all so obediently followed each other to the train. My colleague from the Post Office seemed to have known that things were not as they seemed, but still he had followed the crowd without a fight.

Why?
I was hungry, but I thought it would be best to save the rest of the dry bread for later.
I chose to bury the bread under my pillow, just like I used to hide my book when Father popped his head around the bedroom door to check that I was asleep and not reading.
I laid back on the cloth covered, straw-filled mattress and took in the noise and confusion around me, the strangers sharing my bunk were not anyone I knew. My friends had been allocated to the other buildings. It was all so claustrophobic. The daylight began to darken, it must have been late evening, my eyes closed without any conscious decision on my part. I was briefly disturbed as some of the other prisoners shouted at a prisoner who was peeing off his bunk. At least I had made a good decision by choosing a top bunk. I drifted into a deep sleep, feeling as though I was falling down a deep well. I dreamt I was running along an echoey stone walled corridor in a dark place. I saw my father looking at me, Mother was there, pulling me back by the hand. I broke free of her grip and came face to face with a rifle barrel aimed at my head. I held my breath, I could feel the cold hard metal pushing on my forehead. I heard a bang and saw a bright white flash of light.
I woke with a start to confusion around me. Men were shouting "Rause! Rause!" We were being shouted at by the SS German guards. Other men in soft hats wearing an armband were hitting people's feet with sticks as they lay in their bunks. There was very little comfort in the hard bunks, but it

was so hard to get up. I felt exhausted.

I swung my pained feet to the floor. I was hit by a stick on my arm and back. I had a flashback to when Mother used to chase me around the kitchen, table hitting me with her tea towel for being naughty. I would stop and turn and try to hold her flailing hands to kiss them and apologise for being naughty. That usually made her melt. Today there was no stopping the savage rain of blows on my body and head. A man in front of me stumbled and fell, I recognised the thief stood over the top of the man on the floor. I thought the thief was going to help the old man up off the floor, but no, he started to kick and then hit him with his stick. The man on the floor tried to get up, but was kicked hard again, his breath violently kicked out of his chest by the violent impact. He slowly raised up on to his knees. The thief was signalling everyone to pass by. The old man's face was creased in pain and helplessness, tears running down his cheeks, crying like a young child, looking up at us. I grabbed his arm and pulled him to his feet. No one else helped. There was no kindness in this place, only fear.
I needed the toilet, I pushed my way into the busy toilet area. The toilets were in open rows, no privacy. They were already covered in faeces, peoples digestion had reacted to the nervous strain of being in this horrific place. I would hate to think how the cleaner will tackle that I thought. The steam rose from our urination in this cold place. The smell of *scheisse* filled our nostrils. We

attempted a quick wash in the long communal basins, we were allowed very little time to do this. I wished I was safe at home at the tenements. Home always felt safe even in these recent uncertain years of war and occupation. Even during the Uprising, I would return home to the basement cellars after helping the wounded soldiers and would be embraced lovingly by my mother and father.

At last breakfast. I was so pleased, I was starving. I had not had anything since my bite of my expensive bread yesterday evening.

We waited in a queue, waiting for our breakfast. Breakfast was contained in a big metal pan; it was mint tea. You were allowed to dip your mug in as many times as you liked.

At the sound of a gong, all the prisoners stood up from their breakfast of mint tea, we were hungry. We all exited the front of the building, I felt so vulnerable in my thin pyjama style striped trousers and jacket. It was barely light, it was so cold, I could see the steam from my own breath. The rest of the people in the line looked like they were smoking, as steam from their breath lingered in the cold morning air. We all shuffled closer together trying to use each other's body heat to keep warm. The smell of human stale sweat and rancid breath invaded my senses. I must smell as bad as the others I thought.

Even though they could not move forward due to the number of people in front of them, they were still pushed along and shouted at by the Kapo and SS Soldiers. The prisoners were being conditioned to obey. The best way to control a large crowd is with fear. These evil men were enjoying their reign of power.

Slowly we shuffled forwards in our wooden clogs. We were organised into groups, each group were issued with chores. The queue then continued on to a large open area. Another armband man shouted. The armband men were Kapos. A Kapo is a prisoner like we were, but were given the authority to control the other prisoners; they were given an armband to show their status.

I noticed the smoky air, there had been a smell of smoke ever since we had arrived.

"What's that awful smell?" I asked the others.

A man answered my question, in a matter of fact way, there was no emotion in his voice.

"That's the Jews."

"What is?" I replied.

"The Jews burning. The Germans have the furnaces running day and night in an attempt to dispose of the bodies. They gas the Jews then burn them."

"So we are all going to be gassed?" I gasped.

"No, looking at your tunic badge you are a saboteur. You would be shot, only the Jews are gassed."

He laughed as though he had cracked the best joke ever.

I know laughter is good for you and can make any situation feel better, but no, not today. After what he had said I felt like I would never be able to laugh again.

He regained his composure from his laughing fit,

then continued, "You will have already passed the Angel of Death when you arrived at the camp. He stands and judges whether you live or die, simply by looking at you."

"The thin man with shiny boots and a cane?" I asked, remembering the encounter with the gloved SS soldier.

"That's him," he replied "hopefully you will not see him again, he works mostly at Birkenau, over there, a couple of kilometres from here. He specialises in Jews and Gypsies…Do you know what I mean?"

"You will notice that all the personnel here are SS, they have all sworn to the SS oath of allegiance, the oath pledges personal loyalty to Adolf Hitler the Nazi leader."

He looked a hard man, as though he had seen a lot of bad things and could do bad things to you if you crossed him.

"How do they gas people?" I asked in horror, hardly believing what I was being told.

" There are shower rooms. Poisonous gas is pumped in to the rooms instead of water."

He appeared void of any feelings. All the inmates would become desensitised overtime by the events that they would witness at the extermination camp.

"Rause! Rause!" ordered a soldier.

"Must be time for us to move." The SS guards shouted to get everyone moving.

"Time for work" the guards shouted.

The toil was hard, my hands were soft and bled easily.

"Your skin will become tougher over time" said the laughing man. I never knew his name, he almost gave a wink. This was the first kindness I had seen in this place.
My fellow inmates and I tried to find some enthusiasm for the tasks, urged along by shouts from the guards and snarling guard dogs straining on the leash. The dogs looked like they would have loved to jump in and play bite the skinny prisoners.

After what seemed forever, we were regrouped to have lunch at midday. I was hoping there would be food, there had been none at breakfast.
I passed a soldier without a thought, thinking about my lunch, I immediately felt the force of a wooden truncheon hit me in the solar plexus. His German Shepherd dog was going berserk, it was trying to get near to sink its teeth in to my soft flesh.
The guard spoke "You remove your hat and bid good day whenever you pass a Schutzstaffel officer!"
"Sorry Sir" I had no idea, I was struggling to get my breath after being winded.
Thief man had kept that bit of info to himself. At least the guard had kept the dogs teeth away from me.

Lunch was a bit more substantial than breakfast. Only a bit though. A litre of watery beetroot soup. I fished around in the red liquid and found a small piece of white veg, possibly a bit of turnip and one small piece of potato and a bit of potato peel. This

was such a disappointment.
My body was crying out for the average 2,500 calories a male body requires per day. I must have had only had 20 calories so far today.
I had further duties today after lunch, toilets to clean…
"Why me?"

At last we were rounded up from our chores "Appell! Appell!" shouted the Kapos.
At Appell we all stood and were counted by our allocated armband man, the block Kapo. He counted the prisoners, then reported to the Schutzstaffel officer, the SS letters written in the Armanen runes plain to see on the soldier's collar. He stood in his smart clean uniform among the filth and smells that surrounded him. Everyone had to stand still until all the numbers tallied with his lists. It seemed to take forever. It was cold in the twilight, no one had any concept of time, our watches had been taken from us.

This was another classic institutionalisation technique to deprive prisoners of knowing the time of day. Although looking at how this establishment was run maybe it was just theft rather than conditioning.

When the sun lowered in the sky, this was a sure sign it was the end of the day. If it was already dark and you were being kicked out of the barracks, then you knew it must be early morning. Time meant nothing. Time had been stolen from us, time was no longer ours.

Eventually we were all allowed to leave the Appell and go for the evening meal.
This was quite exciting. A piece of dark brown rye bread, weighing a maximum of 300 grams, together with a tiny piece of sausage and a small blob of margarine and a blob of jam.

They left us alone after the food. This was so called 'free time'. I met my friends Jurek, Waldek, Janek and Bernek. It was so good to see them, my childhood friends, we had grown up together at the Warsaw tenements and shared adventures together. A gong sounded at around 8pm telling us to return to the washrooms. At 9pm the gong sounded again for night time silence. We are not allowed to leave our bunks until the wake-up gong.

We would be up for work at 4:30am. Aching, tired, confused and hungry I climbed up onto the bunk. At least I had my expensive piece of bread under my pillow, I was glad I had it now. I slid my hand under the pillow, I tried again, I lifted my pillow in disbelief, the expensive bread had gone!

Chapter 14

Another day passed. Normality was a distant memory, another day of tasks that passed the time until the evening.
It was Appell time. We were made to stand again until all the head counts tallied. Prisoners who had not performed their chores as expected were brought to the front of the gathering and given a public beating. It was getting cold now, the sun was dropping earlier and earlier down below the barbed wire perimeter fence, autumn was with us. The camp commandant stood elevated and addressed the large group.

"Things are on the change gentlemen. This time next year you will be home with your families."

The camp went very quiet. The German soldiers looked at each other uneasily. To call a prisoner a Gentleman was unknown and to be given hope was never known in a death camp.

The speaker was Arthur Liebehenschel, the commandant of Auschwitz-Birkenau Concentration Camp, he had succeeded the original commandant Rudolf Höss. Höss had been a man that had experimented in various methods to accelerate the extermination of Jewish prisoners during his rule at the camp. Even though Arthur Liebehenschel ran a murderess camp, he made improvements including removing the standing

cells; this was a cell where there was only room to stand. He also halted the process of the selection for the gas chambers. This was the procedure that I had encountered on arrival without knowing it. When prisoners with children arrived to Auschwitz, the parents were told to hand over their children. Children under 16 and the elderly were selected for the gas chambers.
This procedure caused so much stress to his SS doctors that those working on selection resorted to alcohol or drugs before starting their shift for selection. The only two SS doctors who coped with this process were Josef Mengele and Fritz Klein. They alone could carry out this selection process without any need for a stimulant. Mengele sent 400,000 prisoners to their deaths in the gas chambers at Auschwitz-Birkenau. He selected 20,000 Jews and Gypsies per month to be killed.
He would stand at the Auschwitz railhead watching the new arrivals. Dressed in his green tunic, immaculate, not a hair out of place, he made his selection as the new prisoners disembarked the train. People directed to his left were destined for the gas chambers.

Unfortunately for the Auschwitz and Birkenau prisoners, word got back to superiors about Arthur Liebehenschel, he was considered by Himmler to be too 'soft' with the prisoners at Auschwitz. Liebehenschel, was replaced by the commandant from the Majdanek death camp, Richard Baer. Baer was not the affectionate sort. He patrolled

with a German Shepherd that was trained to bite prisoners; Baer enjoyed dealing out pain.
The mornings and evenings became colder as autumn passed and winter came. Appell was a freezing experience. Tonight was worse. The headcount did not tally. Again the count was taken. Everyone had to stay stood still, there was snow on the ground. The camp was searched. The SS guards had to report to the smart
SS Commandant at the front, Richard Baer. Baer wore a heavy coat that insulated him from the freezing temperature. Time passed, the prisoners could not be found in the camp. SS Soldiers were sent beyond the perimeter fence with dogs to search for the escapees. It was late in the night now, early morning. Some of the Russian prisoners resorted to stripping themselves stark naked and rolled in the snow to feel warmth, then they put their uniforms back on. The guards hated this unruly behaviour and would beat prisoners that they could get to.

The method of rolling in the snow works by inducing the initial stages of hypothermia. The cold snow draws the blood to the skin's surface, away from the vital organs and gives the illusion of warming-up and produces a burning sensation. Often people who have suffered from severe hypothermia have been found with their clothes removed. The warm sensation can become so overwhelming that it causes people to try and cool themselves down by removing clothing.

The sound of barking dogs and shouting guards heralded the return of the search party. One prisoner was already dead, he was thrown to the ground in front of the Appell. The second escapee was bound to a post. Guards were assembled, their rifles raised to take aim to shoot the man tied at the stake. He had one severely swollen eye which was completely closed by a large red swollen eyelid, blood ran from the cavities in his mouth where a rifle butt had removed teeth. He was left in full view for us all to see. Again it was a warning, an example.
"You see what happens when you try to escape" informed the SS officer, pointing at the dead man laid in the dirt. The ground became darker around his head as the blood mixed with the soil.
The SS officer's breath vaporised, steam rising from his every breath as he spoke, visible in the large bright camp lights. There was a cloud of vapour above the shivering prisoners standing in the cold, it was now over six hours of standing and waiting.

Body heat is lost to the cold crisp air. Hypothermia taking a grip, the shivers, the tight tense muscles, the jaws clamped closed, grinding your teeth in the cold. There is very little insulation granted by the thin pyjama-like uniforms. We stood with bare feet wedged into wooden clogs.
At last, now we can go to bed. There was no sorrow for the men dead on the ground. We had all suffered enough in the intense cold. I remembered Laughing man's words well, "You saboteurs will

be shot, not gassed."
A loud crack from a weapon sounded. Baer, with his Nazi armband on the sleeve of his thick warm coat, stood near the body of the man tied to the stake. The officer appeared to be pointing at the victim, he wasn't pointing his finger, it was his pistol. Another crack sounded. The victim had already been dead, but Baer made sure of it.

All too quickly the gong sounded, the air was cold in the barracks, the stoves were not lit. The guards were shouting their wake-up medley of "Rause, Rause!"
"What have you got under your uniform?" I asked *Laughing man*.
"A blanket" he replied, I don't want to be cold again like we were last night when we were waiting for the escapees. Come on, time for our wash.
I was becoming accustomed to joining the queue for the toilet, then a quick wash and mint tea. Today we had a morning Appell. Today was meant to be a happy occasion, well at least it was for the camp commandant Baer. He stood in his usual place, skis over his right shoulder. It was announced for him by the SS speaker of the day that Herr Baer was off on his holidays. We must all applaud his happy holiday. We all applauded like performing seals, at least the clapping was warming my hands.

Today we were going in trucks to the forest to cut wood to fire up the stoves in the camp. Our stoves

had never been lit, up to present, but anyway we were on a mission. It was good to get away from the camp. The day was cold and crisp, the sun was rising slowly over the trees. We could smell the fresh air; a glorious smell, so sweet. Today we felt warmer with the blankets hidden under our uniforms. There was no protection from the cold in the open wagons. The guards had removed the canvas weather covers to torment us. At least we knew we could not be gassed with the covers removed.
Everyone pressed together to retain body heat, we leant forwards in the direction of travel, bracing against the apparent wind created by the forward movement of the truck.
The truck sped along, the big tyres hummed on the dry road surface; the noise was hypnotic and a comfort, eyes were closed teeth clenched, muscles taught to combat the cold air on our skinny bodies. I had lost so much weight. My larger friends lost weight even quicker than us skinnier guys.
Laughing man had been a gorilla of a man, he was round about the same weight as me now.

The larger person loses body weight even quicker than a thinner person does. Body fat burns off first, next the body searches for nutrients to preserve life, it does this by devouring parts of the body that it can survive without, muscle is broken down and finally its own skeleton and teeth are used for calcium to preserve itself. Gums start to bleed and teeth are lost due to the lack of calcium. Blood thickens due to the lack of nutrients, heart muscle

weakens, bones become porous, all from long term starvation.
The humming sound of the tyres became quieter as the vehicle slowed, we turned off onto a smaller winding road. Now we sat up and looked around; even in bad times the mountains back lit by a red sunrise is beautiful and those forgotten feelings of being a person and not just a number returns for just a moment. We stopped at a wooden five bar gate. The passenger door opened, a sound of instruction to the passenger from the driver, as the passenger jumped out of the cab onto the tarmac below. I could smell cigarette smoke and could feel a brief faint gust of warm air from the cab. The gate rattled and then opened, the wagon's engine noise increased as the driver eased the wagon forward and then stopped again to allow the gate to be closed behind it. We looked down at the soldier, he was young, no older than 18. He looked up at us, we must have been a pathetic site, bunched together shivering in our pyjamas. He blew a puff of smoke in our direction and laughed. He climbed back into the warm interior and exchanged a joke with the other two soldiers snug and warm in the cab, probably at our expense. It didn't bother me anymore what they thought, they had taken everything from me, my dignity, the family gold, my father's watch, my clothes and possessions, my home, family, friends, my hair, my health. I did not have much more to lose apart from my life and that did not feel to be mine anymore.
I inhaled the sweet smell of forest leaf mould; it

made a welcome change from the acrid gagging smell of the corpse incinerating furnaces at the camp. The wagon bounced along over the mud and ruts made from previous visits by the wagons. The soldiers in the cab were more awake now, we could hear their voices which were muffled by the metal enclosure. Let's hope they are in a good mood, so they don't give us a beating for no reason. My belly was empty, but my bladder was full, relieving it would be my first priority. Some of the other older guys had either pissed themselves or relieved themselves over everyone's clogs. That was alright for short-term gain of warm feet, but it soon cooled off and left you cold again. The guards jumped out of the cab taking a last drag from their cigarettes. All three stood in a semi-circle at the front of the wagon, having a good chat about camp life, not worried about us making a bid for freedom. We would have been welcome target practice for them. We would not have a chance of getting far in our 'super-fast' running clogs.
In their own time they came around to the second class section of the wagon. We were still sat close together for body heat.
"Rause! Rause!" It was time to move.
We stood up slowly, our bodies stiff with the cold. I felt like a lizard that needed some heat from the sun to get my body moving, but the shouts from the guards was all the sunshine we needed. We knew that if shouting with venom and spittle firing from their mouths was not enough to stir us, body blows would follow and a lot of rifle pointing. We jumped from the height of the tailgate, I landed on

the floor in a heap, winded. I was becoming weaker every day. It also took me longer to react to instruction. I heard the words but found it hard to make sense of the commands and then even more difficult to move my limbs and to do what was requested. They beat us for not reacting quickly enough. We were finding it increasingly difficult to function on the tiny food rations they provided us with. After my beating I turned to pee on a tree as the others made their leap of faith from the wagon onto the forest floor, all landing in a heap as I had done. We gathered the tools from the wagon and were marched to the trees that had already been felled.

We worked like a group of ants making the large logs in to smaller sections to load into the barrows. Some began to ferry the wood filled barrows to a second wagon that had arrived, tripping and slipping in their clogs, while the rest of us clambered over the trunks and branches and continued chopping and sawing. The second wagon left fully loaded with logs and returned with our lunch. At last it was runny soup time; swallowing the hot beetroot water gave the illusion of being filled but the effect did not last long, it just made me want to pee again. More clambering and cutting brought the golden sunset, the trees began their silhouette display as the sun dropped in the sky behind them. It was strange, I looked forward to going back to the camp, the smelly barracks and my excuse for a mattress, just to get my head down and drift away from this place in my dreams. Sometimes in my dreams I would be back home with Mother and Father. My mother in the kitchen, busy creating a tasty meal of rice, veal, onion, garlic, egg wrapped in cabbage leaves, Golabki. It was one of my favourite meals. My father would be sat in his armchair listening to the new radio which he was so proud of, not everyone had a radio set.

Then I would find my friends in the park skating and Skrawek was there too. Poor Skrawek, how I missed my little dog and loyal friend...

"Rause! Rause!" I was brought back to reality from my thoughts, the sky was blood red again now. We loaded the wagons with the tools we had brought, tools passed back and accounted for, just in case we were going to keep a saw to cut down an observation platform and put a crease in some SS Guards uniform.

There was a shouting competition going on between two of the guards and one of the prisoners, it was *Laughing man* who they were shouting at. The soldiers were pulling at his top, one of the guards ripped his shirt open. Buttons flying off *Laughing man's* pyjama top. They revealed a tightly wound blanket around a skinny chest. His great idea of trying to keep warm. The pyjama thin clothing provided very little insulation against the cold of winter. The blanket had been our idea of a bit of luxury in the -5°C temperature. The soldiers now turned to face me, they told me to come closer. I warily edged forward tightening my muscles ready for the barrage of pain that I knew was coming my way. The soldier tore back the pyjama top to reveal that I also had a blanket.

One guard dragged the blanket off, I spun like a doll on a music box as the blanket unravelled from my body. The heat I had gained was soon lost in the cooling twilight temperatures. I saw a bright flash of light and stars on the back of my closed eye lids, then I felt pain to the side of my face. My ears rang and for a moment I wasn't on this planet, I could not move, I stood there and took the pain. Then I felt the blow to my solar plexus, I involuntarily lunged forward in reaction to the impact from the soldiers fist that hit me hard. I fell to my knees on to the muddy floor, puking up the contents of my almost empty stomach. The wet mud and vomit soaked into my not so clean pyjama trousers.
We had to work, carry out our daily chores and sleep all in the same uniform. I stink. The wonder of it was that we all smelt as bad as each other, no one worried about their lack of personal hygiene. I now felt kicks to my back, directed at my kidneys, they knew how to inflict pain. I instinctively curled into a ball to protect myself. Foetal position seems to be a natural reaction when there's nothing you can do to stop the punishment.
When the soldiers became bored of pummelling my body, they moved on and gave their attention to the other prisoners. I could hear their shouts and grunts as they were given the same lesson. I wasn't bothered about their pain, so long as it wasn't me on the receiving end. I sat up, my tooth at the rear of my mouth felt loose.
The pain was still partly anaesthetised by my bodies self-preserving actions of secreting

endorphins, these secretions open up the opiate receptors, causing an analgesic effect, very much like an intravenous injection of morphine.
My face was starting to swell; the swelling acts as cushioning to protect the injured area. I could taste a metallic taste in my mouth, it tasted like I was sucking a two Grosze coin. I could feel a warm liquid on my chin, I instinctively wiped my chin with the back of my hand, it was the cleanest part of me. Blood was running from my split lip and gums. I spat the contents of my mouth onto the floor, the frothy red mixture of saliva and blood lay on the wet dark mud along with the vomit. It would all make welcome food for the bugs living in the forest foliage. I attempted to stand. My slippery clogs did not help me, it reminded me of when I was learning to skate as a young child, out with my parents in the park on the outdoor ice rink. They used to help me up off the floor when I fell. I tried to push up off the forest's muddy floor. The natural anaesthetic was starting to wear off, I could feel pain all over my body now. My mother and father were not there to help me up this time. No one was there to help, I was alone in a nasty place.
I was far away in dreams, somewhere in a mixture of the beating I had received in the forest, then the face of the escapee who disappeared through the floorboards of the cattle wagon, to escape this hell hole. His face became long and pointy, his moustache became long whiskers, his features transforming in to a rat's face, then I was hitting the rat and then cooking the rat. It smelt like roast

chicken. I was about to take a bite out of its fat juicy rump, my mouth watered in anticipation… but instead I woke to shouts and rough hands grabbing my top, they were pulling the jacket up over my head as they pulled at me, it was all confusion and noise. I was being pulled off the bunk bed by rough angry hands, my bunk mates just looked and stared, they did not want any part of this. I held on tightly to the blanket, feeling that I was more protected with it between me and an angry mob.

"That's not him! He's too young, the man we want is old, in his 50s. This is a boy."

The one with the grip on my blanket was not convinced. He got closer and was in my face, I could smell his rancid breath and his spit splashed my face as he shouted.

I was dropped by Mr. Spit, the mob had seen their prey in the bunk below where I lay.

The shouting started all over again. I got as far back into my bunk as I could go, out of the angry mob's way. My bunk mates grunted disapproval, but I wasn't bothered, I just needed to keep out of their way. Mr. Spit was dragging a body from his bunk, the victim was sliding out of the bunk, falling head first towards the concrete floor, with a lot of help from a very angry Mr. Spit.

On hitting the floor, his head made a loud crack. The group shouted spat at and kicked his body, which lay defenseless on the floor. They were like a pack of dogs, one of the group was gouging the victim's eyes with his thumbs. I don't know what the man had done, but there was no holding back on the kicks and punches. Mr. Spit concentrated on kicking the victims head. The victim tried to curl up in a ball to protect himself. Blood was starting to cover Mr. Spit's clogs. The attacker stopped his kicking and instead started stamping on the blood covered head, whilst others were stamping and jumping on the victim's body. The sound of the kicks and cracking of bone was petrifying. I watched as the body on the floor writhed and cried out, asking the mob to stop. The victim's nose was smashed and bloody, he tried to clear his airways to breathe by spitting out the frothy blood that was pooling in his mouth. It reminded me of the pain and taste in my mouth from when the SS officer had hit me in the face with a rifle butt. He was losing the battle, his body was no longer curled tightly in a ball, it was more open exposed to the stamping clogs. He was losing consciousness, his screams for help had stopped, he was close to death. The bubbles of blood from his mouth and out of what had been a nose stopped frothing. The blood just oozed out now as his breathing ceased. One more stamp on his face and it was all over. His skull was so badly fractured that clear fluid started to ooze from his ear, cerebral fluid.

The group were exhausted after their exertion, they were panting, their faces shiny with sweat from their efforts. They staggered away like drunks after a night out and left the bleeding corpse where it lay below my bunk.

No one said anything. SS soldiers appeared only after it had all gone quiet. They walked over and looked down at the body, no horror in their faces,

they looked at each other, a nod confirmed he may be dead. We were violent people they were looking after, if the same mob set upon them, the guards might manage to bring down 10 or 20 of us, but they would soon be overpowered by the rest of the mob. One of the guards shouted at two of the many prisoners watching, ordering them to dispose of the corpse.
They immediately obeyed, leaving their bunks to drag the broken body out to the front of the building. Another prisoner was told to clean up the pool of blood. Even though it was a hell hole, the SS officers liked to keep everything clean. They were afraid how quickly disease could spread among so many prisoners in a confined space. They were more worried about themselves being infected by an outbreak of typhoid than our wellbeing. The body had left a trail, a wet streak on the concrete where it had been dragged along the floor to the doorway.
A space had been created for a new unfortunate sole to join our happy team below our bunk.

Today there was news at Appell, we were told that a transfer of some of the prisoners to another camp called Buchenwald concentration camp was imminent. We all left Appell apprehensive at the thought of this move. Would it be better or worse moving to a new camp? Even though it was hell here, I always feared the unknown.
I was in the usual huddle of prisoners at breakfast. It was no buffet, just hot mint tea.
  "I've heard of this place" said one of the inmates.

"It's an older camp than Auschwitz, its name means the Beech Forest, it's on the Ettersberg Mountain near Weimar in Germany."

I held my mug of steaming mint tea trying to picture the camp on the mountain. It all sounded very beautiful.

We were called back into the barracks and told to get ready. We would be loaded onto transport in the next hour.

One hour later to the minute we were affectionately summoned by the soldiers, "Rause! Rause!"

There was no goodbye and good luck leaving present, celebrations or speeches. I had not even had the chance to say goodbye to my lifelong friends Jurek, Waldek, Janek and Bernek. We had been together all our lives.

We filed out into the cold and walked four abreast to the cattle trucks on the rail tracks that had brought us to this place. We heaved ourselves into the cattle trucks. That familiar smell of straw, ammonia and wood that I remembered being greeted by when I had left Warsaw. It seemed like a lifetime ago.

There were mutterings, then shouts of abuse in the wagon up near the front, then a fight broke out.

A body was thrown to the ground then kicked and punched, the gang stamped on him until the body became lifeless. The body was thrown out of the doorway, falling in a heap onto the dirt below like a sack of vegetables. It hit the ground hard, causing the dust and dirt to rise around it. This seemed to set off another reaction in the wagon.

The prisoner next to me pointed and conspired with a prisoner opposite us, they both walked together towards the rear of the wagon near the doorway. I looked to where they were heading, I recognised the man. He stood up ready to flee as the mob walked towards him, he was looking around, should he jump off the wagon, he did not look so confident now. It was a Kapo, he no longer had his band of power on his arm. This was Thief man who had taken my gold for a small piece of bread in return. He shouted back at the approaching men, he was trying to use authority to stop the advancing party. He shouted and ordered the two men to stop, they looked at each other, but all they did was grin. The Kapo looked at the guards below him on the ground stood talking. He shouted to them for help, the two soldiers shrugged their shoulders and turned their backs on him, they carried on with their conversation. The Kapo was no use to them any longer. The gang of two, became four men, then six, I saw the punches and heard the crack of what must have been his neck. One of the gang had grabbed his head and given it a quick swing with all of his is own body weight, just like twisting the neck on a chicken at the farm. The body fell to the floor of the truck, limp, no sign of life. He was lucky, it had been a lot quicker and less pain than the death of the previous victim. Maybe the mob had a little respect for this Kapo after all. His lifeless body was heaved and dropped off the wagon through the open doorway. The soldiers moved away from the wagon so that the corpse did not land on top of them. One of the

soldiers called for two remaining prisoners on the ground, walking towards the wagons. He pointed with the hand that was holding a cigarette in the direction of the lifeless body, he made a 'take it away' gesture without any emotion, no different to if he had been asking for a refuse sack to be disposed of. It did not interrupt the two soldiers' conversation. The soldier took another drag on his cigarette and continued telling the tale, their eyes followed the body briefly, but it did not appear to affect their day at all.
I heard a familiar voice shout my name from the back of the truck, it was Waldek. I was so happy I was not on my own, I moved over to where he was stood with the rest of the gang, Jurek, Janek and Bernek. "Maybe we could jump off the truck Czes, one last time together?" suggested Waldek.
"We still have a life in front of us, let's not jump yet my friend" I replied, I never want to lose you again.

Chapter 15

The railway wagons glided through the tower entrance, leaving the sign at the perimeter of Auschwitz camp, *Arbeit Macht Frei*. The irony was that we had worked hard, but we were not free. The expression came from a novel by German philologist Lorenz Diefenbach, in which gamblers and fraudsters find the path to virtue through labour. The sign was made by prisoners and erected on the orders of Rudolf Höss. The sign at Auschwitz has an upside down B, which is said to be an act of defiance by the prisoners who manufactured the sign.

What had happened to my suitcase that was being kept in safe keeping for me? I could have done with the warm coat that my father had given me. Luckily I had managed to buy a Jacket from one of the other prisoners, it was slightly thicker material than my previous top and made all the difference. At least on this trip I did not have to carry the heavy suitcase like I did when I arrived. It was a long journey from Auschwitz in Poland to Buchenwald in Germany, 859 kilometres. No food or water had been supplied for the journey. When I had travelled with my father to the children's summer holiday camps, my mother Helena would pack up a treat for us both to eat on the train journey. My father Piotr would point out the towns and forests as we sped along on the train. The food in the pack up was always my favourite treats.

Today Father was not with me. I wondered if my family still thought about me. I missed my parents so much.

The train was slowing down, we must be nearing our destination. The brakes started to scrape and squeal as the train slowed and then the sound of metal against metal as the train came to a juddering halt on the steel rails. Our skinny bodies lurched forward involuntarily as the train came to a halt. There was nothing to brace ourselves against, except each other. You could feel the protruding bones of the neighbouring prisoners as we pushed together. Much different to our arrival at Auschwitz when we all carried a bit of weight and were wearing our civilian warm clothes. Now it was all bone and rancid body smells.
We were 'rause, rause, raused' off the train. We left the stuffy carriages which smelt of urine, sweat and wood. We transferred onto the road transport trucks. These were covered, I was worried that we might be killed by exhaust fumes. I tried to gain confidence from words I had heard in the past. You will be shot as saboteurs, not gassed. I remembered my conversation with *old Laughing man* at Auschwitz, he was not with us, I wonder if he will miss us? Probably not, *Laughing man* was made of stronger stuff than me.

We were driven through the town, we could see glimpses of everyday life going on. People in normal clothes, women with lipstick and hats. Men in suits. They all looked so well and plump and wore comfortable leather shoes. It suddenly came to me. So that's why we have the covers on the wagons, the SS don't want to show off how ill we look to the town's population. The wagons started their climb out of the town, their engines laboured on the gradient of the steep climb up the mountain. The journey must be coming to an end. We were slowing down. The wagons approached the camp, the gates of this camp had the words '*Jedem das Seine*' above them. 'To each what he deserves'. "I don't deserve any of this" I thought.

We walked from the transport in procession, four abreast marching towards the accommodation. Buchenwald had all wooden barracks, unlike Auschwitz I, which had a lot of brick barracks. The barracks here had windows at low level, so we would be able to see out. The bunks were also made of wood, three prisoners to a bunk, no privacy. As a prisoner not only is your freedom removed, but your dignity is taken from you also. You are no longer a person, just a set of numbers. This was a big camp. We were told that there was a lot of important work being carried out here. There was a stone quarry and armaments work. There was a rail siding that took manufactured goods from the camp to the nearest town. I was told by the other prisoners I met to keep strong, weaker prisoners used to disappear; that was one of the reasons we had been transported here, to replace the losses.
Weak prisoners were sent to the infirmary hut and left to die. The unable, or too injured to work

prisoners were sent away to Bernburg, which was a state sanatorium and mental hospital. Here there was a special wing that was used to receive "tired" prisoners for Euthanasia. They were sent to the gas chamber and killed using carbon monoxide. The hospital Euthanasia programme was also used to kill adults and children with Downs syndrome, or special educational needs and disabilities also anyone suffering with mental illness, especially Schizophrenia.

The following day the procedure was similar to Auschwitz, we made our way to the communal toilets, mint tea and off to work.
As I walked about the camp I saw for the first time prisoners in uniform. British Airforce, the RAF insignia winged badge was visible above the left breast pocket; the gold woven wings and crown. They all looked better fed than us, not as skinny as on our side of the fence. It was a good feeling to see the brave men that had been giving the Germans a hard time.
Between July 1937 and April 11th 1945, 238,980 people of various nationalities including
350 western allied prisoners of war were incarcerated in Buchenwald.
The kapo of the barracks made his way over to me, he had a list of names. "Prisoner 90701, Czesław Sowinski?"
 I had my new prisoner number. I was shocked, no one had addressed me by name since I was in Warsaw.
"You are a telegraphic engineer, worked for the

Post Office in Warsaw?" said the kapo in Polish.
"Well, yes I did." I was still not sure if this was a good or bad thing.
"Come with me." said the kapo as he turned and expected me to follow without question.
I was joined by a large group of other prisoners. The only information we received was that there was work for us. We were loaded onto transport. The covered wagons set off. This was luxury to have the covers on, a great improvement on Auschwitz.
We passed a sign for Weimar. Steep pitched roof tops of this pretty village could be seen through the rear opening of the wagon. We sat on bench seating that ran down the length of the wagon, the same as used for troops.
We headed on back into the country. There was no sign of a factory. I began to worry for our safety. Where were we being taken to? I had been told before that I was going for work and ended up at a death camp. What was the plan this time? Were we being taken away to the forests to be shot and our bodies left where we fell?
 The wagons were driving towards a mountain, we entered a tunnel that took us deep in to the mountain. We looked at each other in wonder and surprise. What is this place?

This group of prisoners were unaware of the pain and loss of life that had gone in to creating such a vast underground factory, Mittelwerk. The name translates to 'Central Works'; the factory was built in a cavern that had been excavated beneath the

Kohnstein Mountain.
It was during October to December of 1943, about 12 months before my incarceration, that the most physically punishing work had been done by the Mittelbau-Dora concentration camp prisoners; they had struggled under terrible, inhumane conditions to enlarge and fit out the Mittelwerk tunnels. Prisoners drilled and blasted away thousands of tons of rock, they built rickety, temporary narrow gauge tracks to support the multi-ton loads of rock that was extracted from the caves. If the skips or small rail cars, full of rock fell off the tracks, which happened frequently, prisoners were kicked or whipped and beaten until they had re-railed and reloaded the stone into the rail trucks. The prisoners were made to eat and sleep in the tunnels where they were carrying out the excavations. Thousands of workers were crammed into stinking, lice-infested bunks, stacked four-high inside the tunnels at the mouth of the main Tunnel A. They lived in an atmosphere of thick choking gypsum dust and fumes from the blasting work. The work continued 24 hours a day. Prisoners had no running water or sanitary facilities. Dysentery, typhus, tuberculosis and starvation were a constant cause of suffering and death for those unfortunate people. The detainees worked on 30 foot scaffolds, using picks to enlarge the tunnels. Workers became weak from the tremendously physical tasks; working hard on only small rations of food, many became too weak to continue and fell to their death from the scaffold where they worked from. The unfortunate souls were soon replaced by more

detainees. Life was cheap.

People were incarcerated at the camp for very little reason. Some petty criminals, and so called work shy individuals, along with government officials, political prisoners, Jews and pacifists were all gathered up, taken from the streets and sent to the camps to work on the perilous excavations.
Trucks bearing piles of corpses left the work site every couple of days on their way to constantly burning crematorium ovens at Buchenwald.
All of the heavy manufacturing equipment, came from Peenemünde, a military research centre located on the Baltic Sea. All the equipment, on its arrival at the mouth of the tunnel, had to be manually handballed and later installed in the tunnels. The workers used hand-carts or block and tackle to lift and move the heavy machinery. They physically dragged and pushed the heavy equipment along using skids and the on temporary narrow gauge rail line.

We came to a halt inside the tunnels. Soldiers came around to the back of the wagons, shouting at us to dismount from the transport. We were organised in to groups of ten and taken to factory style production lines. Luckily for us the construction and installation was now complete. We had been unaware of the struggle that had gone before us. Now everything was clean and sanitised. Scientists in lab coats showed us the detailed work of what was expected. Intricate work to fit and connect cables creating circuits, to work timers and detonators. This environment was now cleaner and safer to what it had been at the construction phase; a welcome comfort to the new group. Here there was technically detailed work and a warmer environment, this was a refreshing diversion from the camp life we had become accustomed to. The reality was that the new group of prisoners were unknowingly working on the assembly line of a new invention, the Vergeltungswaffen (V), meaning the reprisal weapon. This was an unmanned rocket filled with explosives; the world's first long-range guided missile. It was calibrated to fly by pulse jet engine, the V1, or a liquid fuelled ballistic missile the V2. The missile was sent from German occupied territories to fly to a point over one of the allied cities, London, Antwerp and Liège. When the fuel was spent, the flight slowed and the bomb would fall to the ground and explode on impact.

Wernher von Braun was one of the German engineers at Peenemünde Research Centre, where all the research for this weapon had taken place. His rank was a major in the SS. He led the design and development of the V-2 Rockets; the first man-made object to travel into space crossing the Kármán line. After the War, Wernher Von Braun was a leading figure in the development of the Saturn V space rocket for United Aerospace. The Saturn V space rocket was designed to take astronauts into space. This workhorse of a rocket later transported the space station into orbit; a very different use of Wernher Von Braun's skills.

At the end of the day the team was rounded up and taken back to camp. This camp Mittlebau KZ, previously known as Mittelbau-Dora, was close to the cavernous factory. That night in our bunks, we could hear and feel the vibration from the bombing by RAF bombers. The bombs hit the camp, which was thought by the allies to be army barracks and an arms factory. Their mission was to destroy an arms factory containing the V1 and V2, known to the allies as the Doodlebug or Buzz bomb. However, due to the location of the factory, enclosed in a mountain, it was undetectable from the air. The SS guards supervising the camp and its captives, disappeared for cover as bombs fell on the camp. The prisoners reacted quite differently to the SS soldiers.

With no guards present, we could get out of the bunks and look out of the windows. We had some freedom for the first time since our incarceration. We cheered at every sound of an exploding bomb. The closer the bombs fell, the louder we would cheer. We, the prisoners, had no fear of the bombing raid, we wanted this war to be over.
I remember thinking that night whether we would be home soon. I slept contently that night and drifted off to a better place, skating at Warsaw Park's outdoor skating rink, my father was there, Waldek and even Skrawek. Next I was looking in a shop window with my father next to me; we were both looking at some shiny new skates, how wonderful they looked. "Can I have them as a

Christmas present Tata?"
The shop window transformed into the barrel of a rifle, I could smell the alcohol on an old man's breath, his face was at the opposite end of the barrel. I waited for my angel to rescue me, the immaculately dressed SS soldier. But not this time, he did not appear. A shot fired, I saw a flash of white light, the ground beneath me shook. I woke as our bunks vibrated violently because of the impact of another aerial bombardment. The bombing had started again whilst I had been sleeping.

We lay listening to the deafening explosions. Bombs weighing 22,000 pounds, raised great mounds of earth into the air, crushing and splintering many of the timber framed barracks. The bombers were trying to search out the weapons factory, but with little or no effect on the structure which was hidden deep within the mountain.

Each bombing raid released the same amount of energy as 300 of nature's best lightning strikes. This was a really determined effort. Surly there will be no work at the factory tomorrow I thought. We were woken in the early hours of the morning to the usual alarm call of the gong and shouting guards, which we were now accustomed to. We all made the usual toilet stop. I was now used to the lack of privacy of in the toilets, nobody took any notice of each other. We made our way outside to stand in line to leave the barracks. There was a lot of damage visible in the camp, caused by the

night bombing raid. The wooden barracks that had been standing when we had entered the camp last evening were now matchwood on the floor. The occupants pyjama uniforms were covered in dust and debris caused by the bombs and incendiaries that had fallen on the camp, the result had been many casualties among the prisoners.
Nonetheless, it was business was as usual. A party of prisoners was already onsite, moving debris and lifeless bodies. We were loaded onto the already waiting transport and were sent on our way as if nothing had happened.
The wagons entered the tunnels, everything was intact, untouched by the bombardment. We could not believe that anything could have survived the intense air raid. My mouth was still aching from when I was hit in the face with a rifle butt by the angry soldier back in the forests near Auschwitz. I hoped it would go away. I did not want to report sick, as it seemed to be a one-way street when you entered the hospital at the previous camp in Auschwitz. I had heard others talk about torture and experiments in the hospital.
The pain had become unbearable. I told Waldek about my pain, who tried to reassure me.
"You should be okay, you are young and healthy. Remember they need your skills here. So long as you are useful, you will be allowed to survive."
On this advice I summoned up all the courage I could and told the kapo of my pain.
I was escorted to the camp doctor who inspected my mouth.
"You must have a lot of pain." said the SS doctor.

I had never been so close to an SS lapel badge, it was visible under the doctor's white coat. The doctor sat at his desk and began to write out a transcript of what had been diagnosed in the surgery.

Chapter 16

The following morning I was taken alone by two SS soldiers to a separate wagon. No other prisoners were going on this trip with me. I was not sure if this was a good thing. The two SS soldiers sat in the cab up front, whilst I was in the rear as usual. We drove down the mountain road to the town, which was visible below the clouds. I could see a steeple pierce its way through the lazy morning cloud that held onto the lower mountain tops as though the cloud was sleeping and not ready to rise up or move on away from its cosy spot attached to the mountain and rooftops. It was quite an adventure to be out without the rest of the prisoner group. The two guards were quiet, taking in the scenery, just like I was doing. We drove through the narrow streets, people were going about their business, just like people do in normal circumstances. The wagon slowed and stopped. The driver turned off the ignition. The soldiers climbed out and stretched their legs, exchanging some morning chat. I sat in the silence, looking out at a world that was so different to that of my own. One soldier moved back to the rear, he opened the tailgate and motioned at me to follow, there was no shouting today. I stood between the soldiers, with one at each side, as we marched into a high roof pitched building, it had white painted render walls. Everything looked and smelt so clean. No smell of sweaty bodies. Everything was so tidy, clean and sterile. Nothing broken, no barbed wire or barking dogs. Very much like what life used to be like at home. The silence was unreal, no screams of pain, no shouts of anger nor wheels clattering across rough uneven ground, no barrows loaded with corpses, arms and legs hanging out of the wheelbarrow. I could not believe that some people's lives had not changed during the War. I was marched to a bench seat in the waiting room. We, all three, turned together and sat down at the same time as though we were in a six-legged race, I was thinking of what a strange spectacle we must look like to the civilians in the room. The other patients in the room looked away if they caught my return stare. They were avoiding eye contact with the beast from the prison. The inhabitants of the town never knew the truth about us. They had been told that the people in the camp were all dangerous vicious murderers. The bench that we sat on was padded, I could not feel my ischial tuberosity, the sitting bones of my bum, on this padded seat. Normally sitting on a hard seat I could feel the pelvic bones pressing on my skin. My buttocks were now so skinny that it was painful to sit on a hard surface for any length of time.

It was wonderful sat in a cosy environment, I wished it would not end. All too soon our posse was summonsed to go in to another room to see the dentist. I sat in a comfortable reclining leather chair, which creaked as I positioned myself in the soft leather. Again the comfort was such an experience of delight. Bright lights were positioned above my head, just like camp search lights. A hand above me angled the beams down towards my mouth. The dentist spoke gently, quietly to me, carefully inspecting my mouth with a gentle touch to turn my head. I was not used to being treated as a human being. The tooth was extracted without anaesthetic, but the dentist was very quick and efficient, so I felt very little pain. I didn't think that so much care would be given to a prisoner. Why was the dentist so kind to me? The dentist had no reason to be so careful and kind. I did not want this special treatment to end. As the chair was returned to the upright position, I was reluctant to give up the comfort of the padded reclining chair. I knew when I stood up I would be walking away from this paradise and returning to a scary, harsh environment. A world of pain, noise, filth and death. I looked at the kind human being that had treated me with such dignity and said in the little knowledge of German that I had picked up at the camps, "Danke schön."

The dentist smiled back like a sympathetic school teacher looking at a vulnerable small child.

"Bitte schön" he replied, still looking into my eyes as he spoke, as if he knew what pain I was returning to.

I stood for a second too long, entranced by this unfamiliar kindness.

"Komm her" said one of the guards, breaking the magical spell that had me transfixed.

That makes a change from the usual command of 'Rause' I thought. Even the SS guard's behaviour was kinder in this normal environment.

We re-entered the waiting area, all eyes turned to the group of three. What were the people in the room thinking, did they hate me?
A small child looked up at me and smiled, holding up a toy wooden revolver and pointing it at me. I looked down and smiled at the child. A protective mother grabbed her toddler by the arm and pulled him close to her, away from the pyjama monster. I could see the fear of the mother, which was now mirrored in the child's eyes. The child started to cry, this broke the awkward silence in the room.
I could smell an antiseptic minty scent on me, it was divine. I reached up for a handhold on the wagon and heaved myself onboard. The wooden bench felt hard and cold through my thin pyjama trousers. I looked back at the well-kept white building where I had been treated with such respect. The buildings reminded me of the houses in Szczyrk, where I used to go to summer camp. The wagon roared to life, gear engaged, and with a lurch forward we were off back to our world of barbed wire fences. We climbed the mountain road. The clouds had all moved on or burnt away in the glorious sunshine.

All too soon we were back at the camp. The Red Cross parcels were ready for distribution when we arrived, we would receive them after the evening Appell, during our free time after 6pm.
The prisoners had been allowed to receive parcels from their families since 1942. The main reason for this being the fact that the Third Reich was facing a very difficult situation of hiding the

stories of abuse and killings from the outside world. They also wanted the slave labour to be as effective as possible. However not all prisoners were treated equally; Jewish or Soviet POWs would not be allowed to receive parcels. The parcels usually included things such as bread, butter, onions and garlic. Unfortunately the kapos and other functionary prisoners would open the parcels and help themselves to whatever they wanted, before distributing them to the rightful recipients.

I told Waldek about the dentist and not having an anaesthetic, he laughed and told me I was getting soft.

Chapter 17

April 7ᵗʰ 1945

Today there was a change of routine in the camp. We were not taken to the factory for work. Instead, we were all stood at Appell. For the first time ever, all prisoners were issued with warmer jackets. These had never been seen by us before. I could have done with the this jacket on the many cold nights when we were kept standing waiting for hours until the eventual recapture of escapees. We had always been so cold that we had jumped on the spot, rubbed our bodies with our hands to try to warm up. Our feet were numbed by the biting cold; our wooden clogs did not keep our feet warm in the slightest. We often fell asleep on our feet, our senses numbed by the freezing rain.

It was announced today that we would be walking to Bergen-Belsen. This was a death camp in Northern Germany. What we were not told was that the camp was over 200 km away. We walked for 3 days. We were all very weak, it may have taken even longer, most of us did not make the distance.
Even though we knew our walk was to another death camp, we felt a sense freedom, in the knowledge that the allied forces were getting closer to us. The large guns fired by the allies at the front towards the German troops could now be

heard in the distance. The sounds of the war front were getting closer to us.
At this moment in time, the SS was emptying its camps, there were 30,000 prisoners being forced out of the collection of concentration camps. We were all being sent on a death march away from the advancing forces. About a third of the prisoners would die during the marches.

We were marched out of the camp four abreast with guards at the front and rear. We could see the SS guards, who today were acting very differently. They were not as confident as usual. Some of them had lighter coloured trousers to their usual uniforms, visible below their overcoats. There was a sense of nervousness and urgency amongst the SS to commence the march. They were visibly made uncomfortable by the news of the advancing allied forces. We the prisoners was exhilarated. Whether it would end well was unknown, but we all felt the end was definitely approaching. We were no longer alone, the allied forces were closing in on our violent captors.
My lifelong friends from the tenements of Warsaw were nowhere to be seen. I worried about them.

We seemed to walk forever, the days were endless. We slept on the cold, hard ground.

We were woken by the SS soldiers kicking our legs and shouting, lots of shouting. Some of us fell, the fallen were shot for not keeping up by the SS soldiers' Mauser pistol. We looked around,

some of the SS soldiers were removing their overcoats to reveal civilian clothing. One by one they ran into the nearby forest. I looked at the prisoner next to me his head was down, his breathing heavy.
"Did you see that? Soldiers running in to the woods" I asked.
"Yes just keep your head down, don't draw attention to yourself, the SS are so edgy today" he replied.
"I can't see any guards, should we make a run for the forest? We are so close to the trees, look just there!" I asked again.
"No!" he retorted, "You will be shot. Can't you hear the guns shooting in there?"
I could hear shots in the forest where the SS soldiers had disappeared into the dark woodland. We didn't know who the shots were directed at or what was happening.

We walked through the endless days until we saw barbed wire perimeter fences and guard posts. We had reached a hellhole that looked even worse than the death camp I had first been taken to at the start of my nightmare at Auschwitz. It was far worse than any other place that we had the pleasure to reside at. The prisoners in this place looked in bad health, even worse than us. Many were laid down, near death or already dead. We were taken through the gates and entered the camp. It was all mud and bodies. We were ordered to sit and wait for a food convoy that was on its way. We did not argue, we were exhausted after our march. We were now a

much smaller group than the many prisoners that had set off from the Ettersberg Mountain.
From where we sat on an elevated area, we could see the road disappear down a gradual gradient, it then levelled out as it continued onto the rolling hills in the distance. We waited with great anticipation; we were so hungry. We had never received a convoy of food before. I had lots of time to look around at the group, they had eyes fixed on the backdrop of the rolling hills. Everyone looked emaciated, did I look like that too?
We could see smoke emissions in the distance from a group of wagons, the exhausts were blowing out black smoke, labouring with the heavy loads of our food. I could imagine rosy red apples, steak, bread…

 A dot suddenly appeared above the wagons on the horizon, quite low, well below our position. As it got closer it grew larger. It was approaching fast. There was an explosion at the rear of the convoy, we could see the plume of smoke before we heard the explosion. Clouds of dirt rose into the air above the wagons at the rear of the convoy. All as one, we staggered to our feet. No, this could not be happening. Our saviours, the allies, were attacking the food convoy. The pilots didn't know that this convoy of food was meant for us. We were all starving to death. These well-fed pilots could pull up on the joystick and head for their home base whenever they want, where they will have lots of steaming hot food, warm showers and cosy beds all to themselves.

This could not be happening, this must be another one of my nightmares. Was I awake? Was this really happening?

"Zatrzymać…Stop!" we all shouted together. It reminded me of being at a football match in Warsaw, watching Stanley run for the goal, we were all shouting as one voice.

The US P51 mustang fighter planes did not stop their mission, they continued to drop bombs and fire bullets. We could see the lines created by the huge 30mm bullets kicking up plumes of dirt on the roadside, flames were spat out of the wing mounted cannons as they flew over a second time above the twenty truck convoy. That's all it took, their work done. They climbed and turned, heading off back to base, all flashing perfect white teeth through wide grins of happiness at a well-executed job.

We all sat down together in unison, again like a crowd on match day that had just seen their favourite football player miss an open goal. Heads in our hands, we were all in shock. Then the shouting and wailing started. These pilots had just sentenced us all to death. Without food we would surly die, just like the other prisoners that lay in the dirt of this camp. Corpses lay all around us. The stench from the putrefied flesh was so bad. Figures in the distance could be seen writhing in the flames of the burning convoy, their screams could be heard from where we sat, some soldiers were still trapped in their cabs. I had no feelings for them, I just wanted my food. Maybe we could

allies. We will move forwards towards the noise of the guns" the soldier instructed.
The allies' bombs and gunshots did not worry us, we would cheer and shout with joy when the allied planes bombed our camp.

We slept until the light of dawn made an appearance. The march had taken its toll, we were exhausted and in pain from the exertion and hungry, so hungry. The soldier kept to his word, even though we were nothing to him. He had not been instructed to stay with us, we were a stinking mess. Even so he was still with us, he could have run away in the night, he could have even walked away, we did not have the strength to chase him. He could have left us all to die, we were all not far from death. Dehydration would kill us before calorie deficiency, nevertheless we did need the calories to move our bones away from this place. There was no food here, but there was water from the stand pipes. We each in turn held our mouths to the taps to drink as much fluid as possible before we started the final leg of our journey. Were we really heading to freedom or to our death? Either way it was okay with us, we did not want to die in this stinking death camp. Our destiny was in our own hands for the first time since this war had started.

The soldier stood up when he thought we all resembled something along the lines of being ready. He stood still and just watched the sad sight in front of him, probably just another nightmare being stored in his brain. It was the same for all of us, the nightmares we all experienced in the early hours, at a time when you felt most vulnerable. When you are at your lowest ebb, your heartbeat slows, your body temperature falls, you are closer to death at that time than any other time of day. Maybe that is why the nightmares hit you the hardest in the small hours.

We saw the soldier stood in the middle of what was the Appell area. We looked around at each other, a nod of agreement flowed through the group. Those that had the strength to put one foot in front of the other started to move forward. A sad looking group of survivors. We followed the soldier like the rats following the Pied Piper and walked out of the perimeter gates. I looked back at those still laid in the dirt on the ground, too weak or already dead. We were the survivors, we had to survive to tell the tale, no one would ever believe the horrors that we had experienced. We staggered on, heads down, following the road in the direction of the noise of explosions and gunshots. I hoped those left behind would survive long enough to be rescued by the allies as they pushed on through the front.

We walked until the daylight was leaving us, we saw a farm house set back off the road. We left the track to cross a field and headed towards the farm house, we could see its stables and other out houses nearby. The old soldier turned to us, he told us to wait where we were, he would speak to the farmer on his own. We trusted the soldier beyond doubt. We must have been an unwelcome sight to this poor farmer. The farmer dismissed the soldier and told him to leave, He waved his shotgun first at the soldier then at the mob. We felt no fear we remained where we stood. We were now used to weapons and abuse being directed at us. Two barrels meant only two shots, those were good odds for us, the mob would soon overwhelm him.

The farmer shouted "Kein essen hier." A farm without food? I found that hard to believe.
He said it over and over shooing us away with one hand, while pointing his shotgun at us with the other. He did not have enough food to feed this large group. The soldier spoke quietly and calmly with the farmer. The farmer looked at each member of the group, all of whom had their eyes focused on him. The farmer changed his stance, the shotgun barrel lowered slowly and pointed at the ground; he knew there was no way out of this predicament, he was going to have to give in and give away some of his precious produce. He finally nodded at the soldier in agreement. The old soldier told us to take shelter in the barns while the farmer would try his best to give us some of his food. His wife appeared from the farmhouse and busied herself by pumping a stand pipe. The water poured into barrels, then milk was added from milk filled churns, mixing the milk with the water to make the precious milk go further.

The farmer motioned to a group to help him carry sacks of potatoes and barrels of diluted milk from the dairy into the farmyard. Another group started preparing fires to cook the potatoes. We were so happy to see the potatoes. I had not seen a whole potato since Warsaw. As the fires' flames started to grow and dance in the twilight, we threw potatoes into flames. The smell of cooking potatoes filled the air, it was sublime. My stomach ached, my mouth was salivating in anticipation of the feast. We sat down on the cold floor drinking the diluted milk, it tasted so good. The self-appointed cooks around the fires ate with one hand and threw out hot potatoes with the other hand to the rest of the group. The feeding frenzy carried on, it was like a group of locusts descending on the farm, devouring the potatoes as fast as we could; no one wanted to risk leaving feeling hungry. I sat close to the old German soldier. He was wise and kind. He told us how his son had died fighting at the front. The soldier had never wanted to join the German Army, he and his son had been caught up in the war machine by simple geography. The soldier was Austrian, living with his family on the borders of Germany and they had no choice in the matter. He and his son had to join the German Army or be shot as traitors or deserters. The soldier told us that he never considered himself to be German.

Austria had lost its freedom following the First World War and was annexed to become part of Germany. The soldier and his son had been dragged into the Nazi's quest to take over the world and destroy defenseless minorities. He had

no love for Germany. The war had taken his precious and only son away from him.
After he had received the sad news that his son had been killed on the frontline, he no longer wanted to continue the fight. He sat quietly thinking of his loss and how the war had changed his life. I looked at this unhappy man, deep creases on his face and greying, very short hair visible below his hat. He looked to be in his late 50s, older than my father I thought.

I asked the soldier how he had changed the farmer's mind to provide us with food. The soldier was happy to be dragged away from his sad thoughts. He smiled as he answered my question. "Look around at yourselves, you are a scary mob. I told him you were bad men. Murderers in fact and that if he did not help, you would help yourselves and kill him into the bargain!"
We laughed. We did not feel like a dangerous mob. We had been bullied and beaten into submission by the German SS guards for so long, we had lost our identity, our dignity, we were more like an animal than a human. Maybe he was right? Maybe we were a dangerous mob now. We would not allow anything to come between us and our survival. The soldier was a good old soul, he had his own demons and tragedies to cope with, the same as we had. He was the same as us, a man who had been living his life with his family, enjoying happy times, the love and care of friends and family, some sad times, some hard times. He had been dragged away from his life and placed

into a war by the Nazi war machine.

"Do not eat too many of the potatoes," warned the soldier "you have not eaten for so many months, too much food now will not help you."
I tied twine around my ankles to keep the fabric of the pyjama bottoms tight against my ankles.
 I would save some potatoes in my trousers for later. I never wanted to be hungry again. My stomach felt so full, I had not had this feeling of fullness for so long. I had already eaten too much, just like the over indulgence at a Christmas meal. I imagined Mother and Father. My father drying the plates, stood shoulder to shoulder with the love of his life, Helena. She would playfully splash my father with a blob of washing-up bubbles. He would pretend that it was a real drama and stand there with the best shocked expression that he could muster, then he would lean over and kiss her on the cheek.

I looked up at the barn roof. Were we really here, away from the bunks of the camp? Moans could be heard in the night as men held their bellies in agony, their stomachs distended with the process of digestion. Their stomach acids breaking down the starches of way too many potatoes. Many of the group were violently sick due to eating too much. Starvation had affected the efficiency of our digestion process.

The following day we found a large number of people dead, especially amongst the Russian prisoners, who had literally eaten themselves to death. Well at least they had died as free men. The choice had been theirs, their lives had not been taken away from them by someone else.

We drank the last of the milk for breakfast that had been left in the churns from the night before, a real welcome change from the mint tea that we had had in the camps. We started to regroup, ready to set-off. We walked out of the barns and into the farmyard. We left the dead behind where they lay. We were conditioned that the dead were disposed of in the camp furnaces and the living continued to survive another day. Seeing dead bodies around us was an everyday experience, nothing unusual, we had become desensitised to death.
Ahead of us we could see a group of retreating or deserting soldiers walking directly towards us, fleeing the advancing allied troops. We automatically raised our arms to show that we were not a threat and we would not impede their retreat. The old Austrian soldier calmed down the situation.
"Who is in charge here?" demanded one nervous approaching soldier.
"I am" replied the old soldier, calmly speaking to the panicking German soldiers, "I am taking this group onto a camp."
The other soldiers looked around at each other, speaking together in lowered voices.
"You need to get away from here as soon as you can, the allied forces will soon be upon us," advised the Austrian to speed up the decision-

making by the German soldiers. They nodded together in agreement on their joint decision. They continued on their way, making their escape. We had been spared being shot by the quick thinking of the Austrian. He looked at us.
"They will have wanted to save their ammunition to save themselves, not to waste it on prisoners that look almost dead already." He laughed and turned to walk on leading the way.

We were now so close to the advancing front that we could hear the engines of the tanks and transport labouring over the uneven terrain in the distance.
The soldier assessed the situation, there was danger here.
"We are near the front now. We will wait here, the Americans are not far ahead of us now" he explained.
We obediently sat down. We would have done anything he had said, we trusted him implicitly.
I dug out a potato from my stash in my trouser leg. Even though I was hungry, the cold potato was not as appetising as it had been yesterday and anyway, my belly still hurt from indulging in too many potatoes yesterday.
The noise of the trucks was louder now, we could see the trucks come into sight rounding a bend which obscured the rest of the following trucks. I suddenly felt afraid, this was the moment we had all been waiting for, but yet I felt nothing but fear. Should we hide?
The soldier made my mind up for me.

"We will stay here," he instructed, "no movement now. We don't want to risk any unintentional fire from excited advancing allied troops. Wait here, we stay where we are, I will talk to whoever turns up."

Calm as ever, the old soldier kept the group together. The noise of the advancing trucks and tanks became even louder, we could see the smoke from the diesel exhausts. They came towards us at full speed. The leading Jeep was not slowing down, until at the last moment it screeched to a halt, dust and pebbles showered our group. A soldier in the leading Jeep had his arm up to command the line of the convoy to stop.
"Who are you guys? Speak American?"
No reply from the prisoners.
Then one brave individual from our group shouted, "Polski"
"Polski, yep okay. Kowalski come forward, you have some friends waiting to speak to you man."
Young Kowalski came forward speaking good, but not perfect Polish. It had been some years since he had last spoken Polish; it being his second language. He had been born in America, but his parents had moved to America in 1912 leaving Poland prior to The Great War.

Polish migration to America was intense prior to First world war. Polish migrants moved to America with the dream to own land. The poorer people remaining in Poland had very little chance of owning property in the days of communism.

"Who are you guys?" asked Kowalski.
"Prisoners" shouted the Austrian soldier.
Kowalski ignored the soldier.
"Okay, who is the German guy, do you want me to kill him? Give me your pistol pops."
"Nien! Nien! No! No!" exclaimed the group in unison.
"He's with us. He protected us from other German soldiers and he found us food. He's one of us!" shouted the closest prisoner in German.
We were used to answering uniforms in German.
"Whoa, whoa! Polish or American only guys, I can't understand Kraut!" said young Kowalski in an American drawl. "Okay guys, have you seen any SS Soldiers?"
"Yes an hour ago, that way" replied some of the group.
"Okay boys, you all stay here. We'll get some transport ASAP, to take you to the Red Cross… to safety!"
"You grandpa, you're free. Go now, go home," said Kowalski, addressing the Austrian soldier.
"But I want to stay with my friends" he argued.

"Sorry, you can't stay with them. That's not possible pops, go home. It's over for you, you are free. No one will harm you. On your way pops, go, you are free old man, go, go now!"

"Where can I go?" he asked.
"Anywhere! You are free. No one will hurt you." reassured Kowalski.

I felt sorry for the old soldier. He had helped us get this far. Then he was gone. That was what war was like, friendships were short.

More young soldiers in tanks drove up to our group, all dressed in smart uniforms like Kowalski. They were all young. They selflessly handed out their rations, chocolate and cigarettes to the group. "You guys need this more than us." said Kowalski. His voice was no longer clear and confident, he sounded emotional, the sight of us skinny unkempt prisoners must have been difficult to take in.

"For now you must all wait here, you will be repatriated, all of you together. We have transport following close behind. You are safe. Whatever you have all been through and it looks like you have been to hell and back, it's all over for you now. No one is going to hurt you anymore, we are going to make sure of that," he assured us.

We watched the young soldiers get back into the tanks and Jeeps. The vehicles' engines revved as the drivers prepared to leave us. They were heading in the same direction that we had just come from. I was going to miss them, they were all so confident, they joked with us and I felt almost happy. I could feel their strength and vitality pass from them to me. Our whole group had been affected by this encounter; we felt safe somehow, we felt protected, even wanted. Now the soldiers were leaving, some were shouting out that they were on a Nazi hunt.

Kowalski waved, he was in the last vehicle to leave. He turned towards us as they drove away. "Stay here, you are safe here!" he shouted, cupping his mouth to make a loud haler with his hands. I waved back, I felt like my father would have done, waving me off on an adventure
They all waved at us and shouted in excitement. They could feel that they had a new purpose, after meeting us, they wanted to get close to the soldiers that had abused their fellow human beings so badly. Seeing us, in our impoverished state proved that their crusade was just. We all need the reassurance that we are doing the right thing, our meeting had proved that there were evil people out there that needed to be brought to justice. They had now seen the abuse of human beings with their own eyes. Prisoners like us had just been a rumour to them moments before our meeting. We were probably something that their superiors had told them about in a briefing. They now headed off knowing that this was the final chapter of their battles, the enemy was on the run, they all knew that this Second World War would soon be over.

We sat in the dirt and waited, this was unreal. Was it really all over for us? What would happen next? I noticed that the sounds of battle were now moving into the background from where we had come from, it had up until now been in front of us. We heard more vehicles approaching, before we could see them. It was the second group of transport that Kowalski had told us about. The approaching vehicles were sending up great clouds of dirt and fumes from their tyres and exhaust pipes, the cacophony of sound filled the surrounding area.

"You guys are so thin, this is unbelievable. What did they do to you?" exclaimed one of soldiers in the convoy, "We heard the rumours that there were some terrible camps run by the Nazis, but we never knew how badly. Don't worry you are safe now, it's all over for you!"

He was right, it was all over for us, but they the soldiers, still had a war on. The sad thing was knowing that not all of these strong, enthusiastic, brave young men would survive the final push forward. More chocolate and ration packs were being handed out by the kind soldiers from their own rations.

"Stop, stop!" someone was shouting, trying to be heard above the excitement. "No more chocolate or food. You'll kill these guys with kindness. See how they are undernourished, it will kill them, stop now!"

Chapter 18

We were gathered up and driven to a camp. This camp was unlike any other we had seen before. There were wooden barracks and lots of tents set up on lawns. Green grass instead of mud like our old camp, no smell of burning, no corpses. There was a large vehicle with a red cross on it. Was this it? Was it really all over?

We were gently helped down from the transport, names were taken, clean clothes were issued. The clothing was American uniforms. So smart, crisp and ironed. We were allowed to shower in hot water; I could hardly remember the feeling of being clean. My skin tingled and I felt as if I was glowing all over. I smelt good. The towels were enormous and so dry; what a wonderful feeling towel drying your body was.
We were fed small portions of semolina. Not too much otherwise we would die, so we were told. I remembered the Russian prisoners at the farm, where we had eaten too many hot potatoes. Men rolling on the ground in agony, clutching their distended bellies after gorging on the potatoes. The kind old Austrian soldier had warned us even then not to eat too much.

We each visited the doctor and the Red Cross clerk stamped a card, Sunday 11th November 1945. The details taken would be used so that contact could be made with our families. My ID card showed my date of birth as two years previous to my actual birth date. This made me 21. It would make it easier not needing an adult to verify for me, regarding work, travel and finding lodgings.

We had individual camp beds and bed covers, this was luxury.
The following morning we woke up as the sun began to rise in the clear sky, transmitting its heat into the large interior of the canvas tent. The sky was blue and clear, no sign of smoke, no furnaces burning. We looked around at each other not knowing if we were allowed to get up yet.
Where was the gong and the kapo that used to hit our feet with a stick and the SS guard to shout us out of bed?
"Can we get up now?" said one cautious voice at the rear of the tent.
"Are there any guards?" asked another.
"No prison guards. No one is watching us" I said, as I looked out of the tent doorway as carefully as I could, so as not to be seen by anyone outside the tent. It must be true, it's not a dream, are we really free?
"We are free" I mumbled to myself, then again louder, "We are free!"
I could feel my confidence beginning to return, growing in my belly, bubbling up through my chest, then to my throat, "WE ARE FREE!" I shouted loudly.
I closed the tent flap quickly waiting for the repercussions of my involuntary outburst. I waited

for the dogs to start barking, the guards to start shouting, I held onto the tent flap my hand trembling.

A nurse had spotted me cautiously looking out of the tent. She walked over to check that everything was alright.
"Is everyone okay this morning?" asked the nurse, in German.
I had retreated to my bed as soon as I had seen her walking over to us and closed the flap like a startled animal. The nurse pushed her head through the doorway. I noticed how well she looked, her skin was smooth and clean. Her cheeks a little plump and almost pinkish in colour. Her fair hair was clean and pinned back under a nurse's hat. I had not seen such a healthy, clean woman's face since I had left Mother on the streets of Warsaw, when I had left my family to board a cattle wagon. It all seemed a life time ago. In reality it was just over a year ago. My vision became blurred as my eyes burned, tears filled my eyes and overflowed, trickling down my cheek. I could not remember emotion like this, they were tears of happiness, not the usual tears of pain.
"You can get up gentlemen and prepare for your breakfast which will be served in the canteen tent nearby, all very soon" the nurse explained.
Gentlemen, we had not been called Gentlemen since being addressed by the commandant in charge at Auschwitz. I remembered that commandant. Unfortunately he did not last long at the camp.

I wondered if this was all really happening. I pinched my right hand, my forefinger and thumb applying pressure in a nip to the back of my hand, in an attempt to find out if I was really awake or in a dream. The nurse's head disappeared. She walked back from where she had come from.

The whole group were stunned, in complete silence, legs locked, they could not move; they were paralysed where they stood or lay. We looked at each other in wonder. Had this moment really happened? No one could believe their own eyes and ears. Were we really free?

Some of us got changed into our new clothes. I admired my American soldiers' uniform. Some of the others did not get changed, they were institutionalised by their ordeal and felt safe wearing what they were used to, the pyjama uniforms. We waited for each other to gather at the tent entrance, we left the tent together, we were not used to doing anything on our own.

The food was laid out ready for us on long tables; twelve table settings per table, cutlery, the full works. It looked like semolina again, not that I was grumbling, they were looking after our delicate digestive system after all. I wondered if there was any mint tea.

I was still hungry after our breakfast.

"You must take care at first. Too much food can kill you, you know, when you are in a state of malnourishment like you all are" said the nurse that had greeted us at the tent. She was so

confident and kind. We were not used to being cared for.
The nurse stood next to me at the end of the long table. She gently touched the back of my hand with such kindness. It took me back to the tenements in Warsaw, when my mother sat beside me while I ate my meal after a day at school.
"You look tired Czesiek." my mother would say stroking my hand. "After your food, have a ten minute nap before you start your homework."

I came back to the present. The nurse, who I now knew to be called Erika, was still there looking into my disturbed eyes.
"You look like you have had a terrible time. Don't worry you are safe now" she said.
 "Thank you Erika" I smiled.
I was so grateful for all the help from these kind people. I could smell the fresh smell of shampoo and toothpaste on her. I looked back into her caring eyes and felt as though I was diving into a turquoise pool. Our gaze was suddenly broken by chairs moving. The others had finished and were leaving the table.
I walked out of the canteen tent into the daylight with Erika at my side. What a wonderful day. I took in a deep breath of fresh air.
"So this is what freedom smells like" I gasped.
"What does it smell like Czesław?" responded Erika.
"It smells like nothing I can describe. It's sweet, unlike like the camp I was in," I explained. "The camp smelt of smoke, stale sweat and rancid

breath."

Erika laughed. Her laugh was gentle and as comforting as the feeling you have when sheltering under the trees to escape the falling summer rain.

"I have not heard that sound for a long time" I smiled. "I never thought I would ever hear something so beautiful ever again."

Erika's cheeks flushed in reaction to my observation.

"You have your whole life in front of you Czesław," said Erika "the past is in the past now."

Erika looked closely at me, this fragile human being beside her.

We were all allowed to sleep when we were tired; no shouting and no barking dogs, no work to do, no cold water strip wash every morning, only hot showers from now on.

The American soldiers at the camp asked all the prisoners to join them to identify any SS soldiers that had kept them captive. We joined them in their hunt. One day we came across a German bank that was all locked up. One blast from some well-placed explosives and we were in. There was an enormous vault that was already open. "Help yourself boys, you deserve it!" yelled a soldier. There were freshly printed crisp notes of money piled high.

"It's a shame kraut money is worthless" said another of the soldiers.

"Let's burn it" suggested another.

So we did. We had a big bonfire and lit our

cigarettes with German notes.

I stayed on at the camp, which I found out was an ex-German air force base. It had central heating in every room, which had kept the Luftwaffe pilots toasty warm on their return from lighting up Europe on their bombing raids.
The first bombing runs had been over Warsaw, probably from this very base. Later the bombers ventured further as the Nazis took on the world. The bomber aircraft set-off from here to drop their loads over major cities in Europe and later started their raids against Britain.

*

I had learnt to drive the transport wagons and began to drive the people who lived on the camp into the local town for work.
"Come on ladies and gentlemen. Let's get a move on, so I can get you all to work on time." I called.
"Give me a minute Czesław" a female voice replied. "It's a high step onto the back of this wagon. It's alright for you, you don't have a tight skirt to worry about."
I helped the straggler lady onto the wagon, then closed the tailgate. The sound of the closing tailgate reminded me of the German SS soldiers closing me in when they transported us to the forests to gather wood. Even though it was warm today, I shivered when remembering the forest trips.
"Okay, now we're all aboard, let's fly." I called.

I loved driving. I revved up the engine and got the wagon up to speed. My passengers in the back shouted to me, "Whoa! Slow down! Just because you have a bomber jacket on, it does not mean you have to fly us all to work!"

"Ha…okay" I chuckled, so proud of my bomber jacket.

Life was good. I helped out at the camp, no more beatings, some parties and lots of friends. I could not help but think about what may have happened to my friends from Warsaw. We had stayed together through the uprising and two camps Auschwitz and Buchenwald, but now they were gone.

"You look deep in thought Czes. Let's have some fun and go together to a party" said Erika.

"Sounds good to me" I responded, still distracted by my thoughts.

There was lots of schnapps at the party. Someone had got the autochanger record player going, stacked with Shellac 78 rpm records.

"Drink Czes" ordered one of my friends.

"Water only for me please." I replied. "I'm so thirsty. I didn't have time to stop today. Picked Erika up from her home and came straight here."

"There you go sir, your glass of cold water" said my friend handing me a glass of refreshing liquid.

"Thanks" I said, grateful for the glass of cool water.

I raised the clear liquid to my lips and took a large gulp. The liquid instantly stopped my breath. The glass was not filled with water, it was triple-distilled; it was vodka! My throat burned. The heat

receptors in my throat were coated in ethanol, making it feel as though my throat was on fire, my lungs seemed to stop in shock. My intercostal muscles and diaphragm had been disabled by the alcohol fumes. My body couldn't take in the 19.5% oxygen needed to survive. I was fighting for my life. I ran around the room trying to hit myself on the back to clear my airway. Erika calmed me down, she held me to keep me still and told me to relax. It is an easy thing to say, but I just wanted to keep on running.
Slowly my diaphragm raised and my internal ventilation returned to normal.
"That was meant to be a party joke? It nearly killed me" I spluttered.
"Come on Czes, let's go back to my home, it's still early. You can meet my family. They are wanting to meet you, my handsome Polish war hero."

Erika's father Joachim was the Bürgermeister of the local town. He had heard the story of what my surviving friends and I had been through from Erika and she told me that he was looking forward to meeting me.
"Remember to reverse Czes! Not forward. If you go straight forward, it's a long drop to the town down the mountainside" giggled Erika.
"Yeh, good job you said that" I replied. That Vodka had clouded my judgment. Luckily Erika had spotted what I was about to do.
I reversed out onto the main road and drove Erika home down the winding mountain road to the town. The sky was full of stars. The air was so

clear up on the mountain above the towns, far clearer than the city air of Warsaw where I had lived as a boy.
We arrived at the palatial entrance to Erika's home, a pleasing sound of gravel crunching under the tyres of the truck as we followed the headlights along the wide gravel drive. I thought it best to apologise to Erika, "My friends are a bit lively, I think it must be the war that's affected them."
Erika laughed. Her magical laugh, it was music to my ears.
"So long as you are okay now. That's all that matters Czes." she smiled back at me, "You and your friends have a lot of catching up to do on life after your ordeal at the camp."
Erika leant over and gave me a gentle kiss on the cheek before opening the cab door. The internal light flicked on in the cab, no doubt Erika could see how red and flushed my face had suddenly become. I had been taken by surprise by the kiss. Erika grinned, she turned and got out of the cab and walked around to the driver's side.
"Come on. Come in and meet the family." she said hopefully.
"Maybe another time Erika?" I replied.
"Of course, another time. I had a lovely time tonight Czes. Thank you." Erika sounded somewhat disappointed in her response. She turned and walked towards the house. She slowly turned back to face me, her fragile friend, and blew a kiss. She knew I was still struggling with the demons in my head.

Czesław (2nd from the right, back row)

Chapter 19

Erika's father Joachim and her brothers had been incarcerated in the concentration camps just like Czesław. Erika's mother and father had been born in Austria. The same situation as the old soldier that had guided Czesław and his friends after the dive bombing of the poisoned food convoy. Joachim did not agree with Hitler's beliefs. The Nazis would not accept dissent from Joachim. Late in the night soldiers had visited Erika's home, whilst her family slept in their beds. The tall front doors rattled and banged, as if a huge storm was raging outside. Dogs were barking and wagons' tyres wheeled across the crushed gravel driveway. Joachim pulled back the heavy bed clothes, his feet found the slippers beside the bed. He slowly stood up, walked to the window and pulled back the curtain. He looked outside. He had expected this to happen, soldiers had come to arrest him. His sons were in their bedrooms, they had also been woken by the noise and could see what was happening outside. They shouted out to their father.
"They are here Father, they have come to take us." shouted Jan.

 A stout man in a smartly pressed uniform with SS badges on his lapel shouted up at the windows, his voice amplified with a megaphone in his right hand. Lights were trained onto the front of the building, so bright that the light shone through the

windows and around the edges of the drapes.
Jan knocked on his parents' bedroom door and entered.
"We have no escape." he said, stood by the open bedroom door. "They are all around us Father, I have checked the rear, there are dogs and soldiers there too."
The lights shining into the bedroom from outside made Joachim appear as a silhouette to those in the bedroom. He had pulled back the curtain just enough to see out of the window. His wife Helga looked at her lifelong friend, it could not be possible that someone would come and take her husband away. Her eyes began to burn as her tears welled in her eyes and began to spill over onto her cheeks.
"Do not cry Helga," whispered Joachim "they will not hurt you, they are here for me. I have upset them by not agreeing to join their corrupt band of murderers. The man speaking with the megaphone was in my office yesterday and he told me there would be consequences if I did not obey their request to allow our sons to join his Nazi Army."
Joachim opened the window, it was still dark outside, but the birds had already started their dawn chorus.
"Wait!" shouted Joachim to the circus outside. "I need to say my goodbyes to my family, then I will join you outside".
Steam came from his mouth as his words met the cold air from the open window.
"No, no, no Joachim! We want you and your sons" explained the portly SS man, papers held high

above his head to justify his request.
He waved them in the lamplight. They could have been anything, his map, a menu, probably nothing legal, but how can you argue with armed killers?
"No," argued Joachim "just me, not my sons."
At that the SS soldier nodded to two soldiers in tin hats. They shot at the large double doors, the mortice locks shattered and splinters of wood from the ancient oak doors flew into the air, leaving scars in the wood. The two soldiers then shoulder barged the doors to break any internal bolts holding the doors closed. They continued to charge at the doors until the remaining bolts bent and broke under the combined force of a quarter of an imperial ton of man body mass.
"Where is Michael?" Joachim asked his son Jan.
"In his room, I think he is afraid." Jan replied.
"We are all afraid" said Joachim.
Jan had never seen his father show any fear in all the 20 years of his life. He felt lost. His father would surely think of something, he was a man of power in the town. Joachim knocked on Michael's bedroom door. He pushed it open and could see the shape of his son in the shadow created by the arc lights in the driveway. His son's bed sheets were covering his head. The covers where he lay were visibly trembling and the muffled sobs from his petrified son could be heard.
 "Come now Michael, we must go with these people." Joachim said calmly.
The sobs got louder as his seventeen-year-old son's head appeared above the bed sheets. Erika ran across the hallway to her brother's bedroom.

"What is happening Father?" she asked.
"Nothing for you to worry your pretty little head about." he reassured her.
Joachim hugged his daughter; she felt so soft in his arms. "Go to your mother Erika, she will need your support and love."
Joachim and his sons stood at the top of the stairs. The soldiers raised their guns to aim.
"There will be no blood spilt here tonight if you and your sons come with us quietly" said the portly SS man.
The trucks loaded up their prisoners. Barking dogs were lifted into the back of the trucks. Shouts and commands could be heard by Helga and Erika who were now inside the house all alone. They could smell the fumes coming into the house from the vehicles' exhaust pipes idling outside. The double entrance doors had been left wide open. They could hear the sound of gravel crunching as the men walked over to the convoy. The engines changed tone and the trucks all left together.
No sound of shots thought Helga. The SS officer had kept his word, no blood had been spilt here tonight.

*

I met Joachim the following evening as I had promised Erika I would. Joachim looked a lot thinner than the usual Bürgermeister; he was still recovering from starvation like me and my friends. Jan and Michael came towards me to shake my

hand. We looked into each other's eyes. We did not need to speak. We all too well knew of the horrors that everyone in this room had endured whilst incarcerated in the concentration camps.
We all sat down in the wood panelled dining room. I couldn't help but think how this room could have been used to house me and all my friends at the barracks, it was so big. Helga and Erika fussed around the men bringing in even more food. Helga was the image of her daughter, apart from a few lines on her brow and around her mouth. Her hair was identical to Erika's, blonde and wavy. Erika had her father's nose, small and button like.
Erika had told me that she had recounted to her family my story of having been in the concentration camps of Auschwitz and Buchenwald and about the death march that I had also endured. Joachim and his sons understood the hardship, they themselves had been through it also, the beatings and degradation. Being made to feel less than human by their captors. Like me, they too had been incarcerated in Buchenwald.
The women looked and listened as we relived our haunted past. So engrossed in conversation we were all transported back in time to the concentration camps. The smells, burning furnaces, the cold Appell evenings, the cold water to wash in, the mint tea. They all knew it well. The sad separation from their families, laying in the crowded smelly bunks. Not knowing who to trust. Being alone among lots of strangers.
At the end of the meal Joachim invited me to walk outside with him. He had put his arm around my

shoulder, like an affectionate father. The sound of crushed gravel was audible beneath our shoes. It was great not having to wear the wooden clogs in bare feet. Socks made your feet feel so cosy.

"Look Czesław, this could be your new office" Joachim said to me. " I would like to employ you as 'mein chauffeur', I understand that you love to drive."

We were both stood in front of a black shiny Mercedes Benz 600 that was parked on the brown pebble driveway.

"Fantastisch!" I exclaimed.

Joachim opened the driver's side door. The luxurious smell of polished leather filled my senses. The interior was clean and shiny, the windows were crystal clear, no smudges or marks, so clean, it was as if there was no glass there at all. It was in far better condition than the old truck that I was driving at the camp.

"Give it some thought Czesław" said Joachim, squeezing me tight, like a long lost son.

"Yes I will," I replied "I will think about your kind offer Joachim."

Czesław's ID papers issued by the Red Cross.

Czesław in his American uniform at the camp.

Czesław in Germany

I returned to camp that evening, not knowing what to do. One thing I did know was that I could not return home to Poland at the present time. The very thing that the Warsaw Uprising had fought to prevent had happened. Russia and Poland's Communist Party was in control of Poland. Poland's government was still in exile in England and the present regime in Poland did not like the Polish war heroes.

"It is make your mind up time," said Wojciech, one of my friends.
"Yes I know" I replied.

Chapter 20

The Polish servicemen based in the United Kingdom had not been allowed to join in with the 1945 Victory Parade. The British incoming Labour government did not want to upset the Soviets and the Polish communist party who were in control of Poland. What would Winston Churchill have said about that if he had remained in office?

Britain's knee-jerk reaction immediately after the war was to deport all the Polish war heroes. As a result, many Polish servicemen that had fought bravely for Britain were soon repatriated . When they arrived in Poland, they were not greeted as heroes, but instead were regarded suspiciously by the communist government. Many of the servicemen who did return were hunted down by the secret police and the heroes simply 'disappeared'; the Russians had wanted to suppress any Polish nationalism.

The mindset of repatriation eventually changed in the United Kingdom, as it had become clear that it was dangerous for the Polish refugees to return home. Unfortunately it had taken until 1947 for the mistake to be rectified. Britain, along with America, Canada and Australia felt a duty to protect the isolated Polish refugees, taking into consideration their great efforts in serving with them in the war and the bravery of the Polish forces fighting at battles such as Monte Casino in

Italy, as well as the long battle commonly known as the Battle of Britain.

The Battle of Britain was the first military battle fought entirely by air forces. 147 experienced Polish pilots of the 303 squadron, one of the highest scoring of the hurricane squadrons, helped to turn the tide of the determined German aerial attacks on Britain. Winston Churchill named the pilots who took part in the battle which raged for years as 'The Few'.

The reaction to the atrocities in Poland, against the returning refugees, led to the United Kingdom passing a bill in parliament, the 1947 Polish Resettlement Act. This act included the founding of the Polish Resettlement Corps to allow Polish servicemen and refugees to live in Britain with the right to work. The unions, which were powerful in Britain at the time, had an affiliation with Britain's Labour Party, they had to be consulted with regarding the Polish refugees' right to work in Britain.

Britain, Canada, Australia and America needed a workforce following the war and as a result, produced promotional films to show refugees what they could expect when they arrived to work in the country of their choice. The films portrayed the opportunities as being very desirable and offering a great lifestyle. At the end of each working day, the workers were showering in white-tiled pristine shower rooms provided by their employers. It showed people going out together after work, with their friends in the evenings and weekends, with lots of cash in their pockets to spend. It all looked a very exciting life. One of the Polish refugees watching this films was Czesław, back at the camp in Germany.

*

"What about Erika?" Wojciech asked me.
I thought about the question, it was the exact same question that I had been asking myself over and over. Erika was an amazing girl, but she was German. My mother and father would never accept a German daughter-in-law, not after all the hatred and killing. I never answered Wojciech's question and quickly turned the conversation back to him, "What about you Wojciech?"
"I'm going to America. The weather is too cold and wet in Britain for me." he said.
"I like the look of England." I replied.
"America for me. New York, the Big Apple as John J. Fitz Gerald, the sport's writer calls it." Wojciech grinned.

Czesław in Germany, just before he travelled to Guernsey

Chapter 21

The ship docked in Southampton. I had entered a new world.

I started work as a crop picker in Guernsey, on one of the Channel Islands. The weather was so good, Wojciech obviously did not know what he was talking about.

I was stood in a queue in a small convenience store. There was a young woman at the counter, she saw me and gave me a cheery wave. She had never met anyone Polish before. When it was my turn to be served, I looked up at the shelves at the back of the counter and tried to think of the words to describe what I needed to buy today. I tried a little German that I had learnt at the American air base in Germany and in the concentration camps. I suddenly remembered that the people of Guernsey did not like the Nazis, no more than the Polish people did. The Germans had turned up here uninvited and took over their islands.
"I poor English" I said
"Never mind," the young woman smiled "point and grunt or even speak Polish, never speak German to me. I'll help you until you learn some English."

I loved Guernsey, its red sunsets and dry warm weather. The people were so friendly and helped me learn my third language, English. I always remembered to speak English and not German from then on.

The glorious summer days all too quickly passed by, autumn was fast approaching. There was now less work available picking fruit and vegetables on the Islands, so I moved onto the mainland to work in Oxford, again crop picking until the winter.

I discovered from my fellow refugees that there was lots of work available in the textile industry. This was all year-round work, not seasonal like the fruit and vegetable picking business. The big textile producers were in a place called Bradford in Yorkshire, in the north of England.
"The only problem is the climate, cold and wet there. Worse weather than here in the south of England" said Adalbert.
I ignored the advice of my friend and booked a ticket for the train. I was ready to go. My bag was packed, all my possessions fit in to one bag. It was easy to travel when you were a refugee, because you owned very little.

It was a long journey from Oxford to Bradford. I enjoyed being on a train, it always seemed exciting apart from my one trip to Auschwitz of course. I looked at the other passengers and wondered what their reason to travel to Bradford was. I thought about Adlebert's observation about the northern weather. The weather can't be so bad surely, I thought.

I arrived at the Exchange railway station in the city of Bradford; a large station with ten platforms, high roofs with metal structures supporting glass panels. I could hear the rain battering the glass panes, high up on the roof structure above.
Oh blooming! Maybe Wojciech and Adelbert had been right after all about Yorkshire weather. I reached the exit, the sky was black with rain clouds. This was how it remained, it rained constantly for days.

Chapter 22

The bleak moors were covered in fog. This was a cold place thought Maria, or Marisa as her family had called her as she grew up. Maria was from a large family of eight children. Anselmo, Nicola, Maria, Argia, Adolfo, Dino, Rosa and Lina. Maria's aunty was also called Maria, so to prevent confusion Maria became affectionately referred to as Marisa and the name stuck with her throughout her life. The Cioccio family owned a farm near Sestino in Northern Italy, nestled amongst the rolling Tuscan countryside of Arezzo. Marisa, being the eldest of the girls, had the responsibility of looking after her younger siblings. Life was hard, her parents were busy on the farm, leaving Marisa to cook and wash clothes. There was no washing machine; Marisa used the large metal tubs and a washboard to scrub the clothing clean. Marisa darned the worn-out socks and made clothes for the family.

When Marisa reached 17, she realised that farming life was not for her. She spoke to her Aunty Maria and told her that life on the farm was not what she wanted to do for the rest of her life. Her Aunty Maria had a solution; she knew a trusted friend in Florence, who was a dentist and needed a dental nurse.

Marisa left the countryside behind, bound for the capital of Tuscany, where she joined a dental practice and trained as a dental nurse. Marisa enjoyed the challenging work. Romance blossomed and Marisa began a relationship with the dentist's son.

Life was so much better in the city for Marisa, until an unfortunate situation changed her exciting new life. One day, while the dentist was away, a patient in pain visited the surgery demanding a tooth extraction. Despite having carried out this procedure many times before, under the dentist's supervision, Marisa explained that she was not allowed to carry out any dental work without the dentist being present. Nevertheless, the patient in pain pleaded with Marisa to carry out the treatment until she reluctantly agreed.

Regrettably this was a huge mistake and when the dentist found out what Marisa had done, she was no longer allowed to carry on working as a dental nurse and instead was sent to work on the reception.

More tragedy was to follow; the dentist's son, Marisa's boyfriend, fell asleep at the wheel whilst driving one evening and was killed. After the accident, the dentist decided to sell the dental practice and retired. He decided to move to Greece and asked Marisa if she would like to join him and his wife to start a new life in Greece. Although flattered by the offer, Marisa did not want to go to Greece and equally she did not want to return to the family farm. She instead chose to follow a group of friends who were going to England to find work.

Marisa before her departure from Italy to England

Marisa started her new life in England in the land of the Bronte's, Haworth in Yorkshire.

There were more than 300 textile mills operating in and around the Bradford area, making it one of the world's leading areas for wool trading. The industry kept a workforce of 70,000 people employed and the mills produced textiles from wool, operating 24 hours a day. Marisa started in the spinning section. Here, the wool was made into a thread and wound onto bobbins. The bobbins were then used for hand or machine knitting and on weaving machines. The mills were noisy and hot; a harsh environment to work in.

All the girls were so envious of Marisa's stockings that had been sent to her by her family in Italy. The other girls just had bare legs and it was very cold at winter time, especially in Haworth.
"The poor things, their legs were so cold" recounts Marisa. They used to ask Marisa to sell her stockings to them. There was a real shortage of 'Nylons' after the war.

Marisa changed her place of work and moved to the Shearbridge area of Bradford, where she lived in a hostel with a group of Italian girls. At weekends they used to visit Bradford's Lister Park. This was a place where they could meet and talk with their friends.

"Come on Czes, I've arranged for us to meet up with the Italian girls." said Edzio, a fellow Polish

refugee like Czesław.
"Ah ok, did you arrange it with Francesca ?" Czesław asked, looking in the mirror while adding the Brylcreem product to his hair with his right hand, the other hand held the jar. The label boasted "The Perfect Hairdressing." Czesław could see Edzio's reflection in the mirror behind him, sat on the bed polishing his black shoes.

"Yes, Francesca spoke to the other girls at the hostel. She told them that there was another handsome Pole, almost as good looking as me and unattached!" joked Edzio, adding a bit of spit to his already shiny polished shoe.

"Ha, yes. I hope they are as nice as your Francesca" Czesław said. He had his back to the mirror now, checking his jacket for dust specs.
"Let's go! Come on we will be late." urged Edzio, walking to the room door.
"Just give the back of my jacket a brush will you Edzio, any dust specks?" Czesław asked.
Edzio gave a series of brushes over Czesław's jacket.
"Great, you are ready to impress now"
"Ready to go" grinned Czesław, with one eye still on the mirror as he walked towards the door.
As Edzio was locking the room door, they saw another one of their friends.
"Hey Sikorski, we are off to the park, you coming too?" asked Czesław.
"I don't want to spoil your chances with the girls, Czes" laughed Sikorski, giving Edzio a

conspiratorial wink of the eye.
"There is no fear of that, look at me. Tonight I cannot fail." beamed Czesław. He twirled around like a ballet dancer, then stopped with an exaggerated stagger as if he was dizzy.
"Forever the actor." said Sikorski, raising his eyes to the corridor ceiling and shaking his head.

Sikorski had been a paratrooper in the war. He had been in battles that he thought he may never return from. Sikorski had told Czesław about his life as a para. You were dropped behind enemy lines and were always surrounded by the enemy.

They walked together along the main road, following the park wall and then entered through the park gate.
"This takes me back to Warsaw before the war, walking to the park. I used to love skating, I can remember those cold crisp evenings after school." reminisced Czesław.
"Look, there's Francesca and the girls" said Sikorski, gesturing ahead.
"Wow, I love the girl with the long dark hair" exclaimed Czesław.
"That's Marisa" said Edzio.

Marisa

Sikorski, Marisa & Czesław in Lister Park, Bradford

Chapter 23

Czesław and Marisa married and lived together at Ash Grove in Bradford in a rented house of multiple occupation; a large house converted in to flats. Here their daughter Kristina was born. The landlord demanded half a crown, two shillings and six pence more rent when the baby arrived. Czesław was not happy with that, so they moved to Chesham Street. This was a lovely flat with nice neighbours, but the only downside was that it had a shared outside toilet. If you needed to use the toilet in the night, you had to go outside. Czesław and Marisa only stayed there a few weeks, then moved to Richmond Road, where the Bradford University is now.
Czesław worked nearby at Lister Mills; the largest silk fabric producing mill in the world, whereas Marisa worked as a housekeeper for a Catholic priest, Father Taddei at Trinity Road in the Little Horton area of Bradford. Father Taddei later became a missionary preacher in Africa. He kept in touch with the family by letters from his Missionary. They were tenants at Richmond Road, and lived with a young couple, the landlord Paul and his Austrian girlfriend. Paul was Polish, he had served in the German army. There were no bad feelings between Czesław and Paul. The war was confined to history now. Paul's girlfriend was desperate for a child, she loved to play with their daughter, Kristina. They spent many evenings all

together talking, drinking tea and enjoying food.
There was no television as a distraction.
Marisa and Czesław were ready to go ahead and purchase a house from their landlord Paul,but the solicitor was corrupt, he ran away with their deposit and all of his clients money. Marisa and Czesław knew a friend called Janek, a mountain of a man. He located the solicitor and visited the rogue. The money was quickly returned to Marisa and Czesław. They both decided to spend this money on the trip of a lifetime.
Czesław, Marisa and toddler Kristina went to visit Marisa's brothers and sisters who now lived with their own families in Florence. Her mother Pegli Giuseppina and her father Giovanni still lived on their farm in Sestino. This was their first trip to Italy since the war. Czesław loved the early mornings on the farm at Sestino. Especially searching for where the hens had laid their eggs. Czesław used to make a hole at each end of the still warm egg and suck out the contents, raw.
He hated seeing the hens being killed for food. Czesław tried but could not undertake the task of wringing a hens neck. Marisa and her parents, being used to farm life looked on in great amusement at Czesław and his futile attempt.

They told Paul and his girlfriend about the change of plan and that they had applied for a Council property. Paul understood the situation and what's more, Paul's girlfriend had sad news to tell. It transpired that Paul had a wife who lived in Poland with his nineteen-year-old daughter. His wife had decided to come and live with Paul in England, something that he had never expected.

"I am leaving also Czes. I will go back to Austria." said Paul's girlfriend.

Czesław and Marisa were allocated a maisonette at the newly built flats and maisonettes at Parkway in Bradford. This is where their son Edward was born; number 7 Fenwick House, West Bowling.

Marisa, Edward, Kristina and Czesław,
near the newly constructed Thruscross Reservoir
1966

There was one coal fire in the lounge and an electric one bar heater in the bathroom, plus an immersion heater for hot water. There was no other heating in the property. It was so cold in the winter. The settee was pulled up close to the coal fire when you walked behind the settee, the air temperature dropped as though venturing out into the Arctic. This flat was not as luxurious as the pilot's barracks in Germany, where Czesław had central heating. The poor design was common in housing pre-1970 in the United Kingdom; the local authorities up and down the country were charged with the duty to build and provide housing and carry out slum clearances. The council properties built after the Second World War were typically system built, which were concrete constructions with little, if any insulation.

The properties were inferior in build quality to the post-First World War traditional builds made of stone and brick; these properties were built to improve the health of the population. There had been concerns by the recruitment staff about the physical health of recruits that had joined up to fight in the First World War battles. There was a slogan for the new homes, 'Homes fit for Heroes'. The returning war heroes had expected a better lifestyle on returning home from the wars. The Government saw a need for improvement in the housing stock to produce a healthy workforce and physically healthy recruits for any future wars.

In 1969, Czesław, Marisa and their two children moved to a newly built Council-owned maisonette at 21 Ternhill Grove, Park Road, back in the city centre of Bradford. These maisonettes had underfloor heating on the ground floor, but no space heating upstairs. However it was still a great improvement on the maisonette at Parkway.

Both of the council-owned properties that Czesław and Marisa had lived in have since been demolished. They had been the typical quick-build properties, constructed to replace the terraces and back to back pre-war slum properties that still had outside toilets.

Czesław started work at Salt's Mill in Saltaire, near Shipley. The historic village of Saltaire, built in 1853 was designed and built by the philanthropist Sir Titus Salt, from Morley near Leeds.Titus had the mill built and the surrounding village to house his workforce in an open area, with fresh air on the banks of the River Aire and the Leeds and Liverpool Canal, away from the smoke and pollution of the cities. He put in place health care and education for his workers and their families. Along with homes, he provided a school, a hospital, a large park, a congregational church and Almshouses. Anyone who could not work due to infirmity or disease could rent one of the Almshouses.

Marisa became involved in nursing and worked for many years at St Luke's Hospital on Little Horton Lane in Bradford. She was a nurse on the maternity wards and later, she worked on the children's wards at Leeds Road Fever Hospital at

Leeds Road in Bradford. Marisa worked night shifts to provide for childcare needs, which must have been exhausting. Czesław changed his job to become a warehouseman for what was a catalogue giant of the times, Grattan. The workplace was cleaner and quieter compared to the mill environment that he was used to. The Bradford catalogue companies Grattan and Empire Stores were a shop from home concept; they published great big heavy catalogues, prior to access to internet shopping, containing pictures of their products, just like the websites of the present day. They offered credit and items could be purchased in weekly instalments.

Around 1970, Marisa and Czesław purchased their own private house at 82 Woodcot Avenue in Baildon for the sum of £3,500. This was shortly before the first property housing boom, where property prices increased dramatically in relation to income.

The children, as children do, grew up and had their own families. Kristina married Henry, they have two girls, Amanda and Lucinda. Their daughter Lucinda now has two children, Xander and Annabelle. Edward married Julie, they have two children, Kate and Andrew.

Marisa and Czesław later moved to a private flat on Regent Road, near The Grove in the centre of Ilkley, where they both resided until the end. Marisa lived to the age of 84 with many happy memories of playing with all their grandchildren. Czesław lived to almost 90 and was lucky enough to spend time with not only his grandchildren, but both great grand-children; Annabelle the youngest great-grandchild was born four weeks before Czesław passed away on the 25th February 2016, two days before what would have been his 90th birthday. Czesław had his wish granted. His wish? "I do not want to be ninety".

Czesław enjoying his favourite fish and chips at Harry Ramsden's, Guiseley. (Picture taken by his granddaughter Amanda on his 88th birthday)

It's a happy farewell from Czesław at his flat in Ilkley.

No matter how sad the story was that he told, it was always a sad story, told with a smile.

The Author

Edward Sotheby (Eddie), son of Czesław and Marisa, brother of Kristina.

Eddie is a YouTube channel creator and now a printed author. He is the proud owner of Sotheby Swim School, where he has taught swimming for 23 years.

Eddie combines travel with his love for photography, skiing ,scuba diving, sailing, cycling and spending time with his family.

Eddie feels so grateful to be alive. If his father had not been so lucky and resilient to defeat death during the war, Eddie and his family would not be here to tell the tale.

Eddie's Thoughts

Kristina gave me lots of encouragement to start this book and Amanda, my niece, gave me the lovely picture of Dad, Czesław, enjoying his fish and chips at Harry's.

Lucinda my niece kept asking, "When will Uncle Edward's book be completed?" After all, it did take me four years to produce.

My daughter Kate supplied the picture of Dad waving goodbye and spent many months checking

my spelling and reading through the story.
Andrew, my son helped reading through the book.

The title was from something inspired by my daughter's fiancé, Aidan. I am excited to say he is going to be our son-in-law, around the time this book will be published. Aidan told me, "You know, all the stories that Czesław told us, no matter how sad they were, they were always told with a smile."

My daughter Kate and son Andrew loved the stories told by their Grandad and Andrew was with me at the recordings I made of my Dad's voice, telling us both his incredible stories.
Thanks to Father Kieron Walker who read at my father's funeral. Father Kieron was very interested in my decision to write a book about my father and the war. He told me about the murderous Dirlewanger Brigade and their wicked part in the Warsaw uprising. I felt I needed to research this and added it to the book.

The hardest part of writing a book is starting the story. The very first line was written many times over. I kept checking the word count as I progressed and spent hours trying to write down the bare bones of the book, gathering the facts and remembering the amazing tales we had been told as young children. After the death of our mother, Marisa, my father and I spent hours talking about the past, but it was never in any specific order of events. This book has helped me to put everything

into a sequence of when it happened and has helped me see the whole picture of Czesław's and Marisa's life.
I have never written a book before, but I used to enjoy writing essays and a couple of poems, which were read out to the class by the teacher while at St. Bede's Grammar School in Heaton, Bradford.
I love to say I went to 'eaton!

I have read books by author Andy McNab. He writes in such an honest way, pouring his feelings, positive and negative onto the pages. This inspired me to try and write myself and also to jump out of an aeroplane.
This gift from my dear father, the story of his life, entwined with the stories of so many other people of that time, needed to be recorded somehow. I could not let the stories die with me.

This book helped me come to terms with losing my parents. The wonderful thing was all the stories were in their lifetime, before I existed, but I could relive their lives through writing this book.

I hope the book inspires you to write. Everyone has a story to tell. If I can do it, I know you can do the same.

I enjoy media and have a YouTube Channel Eddie Sotheby, as well as an Instagram account @eddiesotheby. I hope to connect with you all on there and maybe you could subscribe to my channel.

55,384 words. I'm so proud of this word count. I did not think I would get to more than 20,000 words.
The legal stuff

This book is copyright material and must not be recopied, reproduced, transferred, distributed, leased, licensed or publicly performed or used in anyway except as specifically permitted in writing by the author, allowed under and conditions under which it was purchased or as strictly permitted by applicable copyright law. Any unauthorised distribution or use of this text may be a direct infringement of the author's and publisher's rights and those responsible may be liable in law accordingly.

Printed in Great Britain
by Amazon